THE
YOGA TEACHER

JULES COOPER

Jules Cooper is a writer and over-educated foodie who lives with her husband Rick in Vermont. This is her third book, after *Birthright Knowing* and *Marcea of the Dust: The Lost Girls.*

∽

The Yoga Teacher

Published by
Price Creek Press
pricecreekpress@gmail.com
Vermont, USA

Cover by 100C

ISBN: 978-1-0881-2738-4

For
Cy, Hope, and Lyris

M OST PEOPLE WHO ARE OLD ENOUGH *to remember the Twin Towers coming down remember exactly what they were doing that
morning. As we watched the endless replays on TV showing the
towers turn to dust before our eyes, we were horrified but couldn't look away.
People inside the towers leapt to their deaths below, tearing at their clothes as
if they were on fire—despite the absence of flames. We watched, and remembered, forever. It is marked indelibly into our psyches and our lives.*

*Everything changed after that day, but if you weren't old enough to know
how things had been before, you wouldn't have noticed the changes. First was
our surrendering to Big Brother intrusion into every aspect of our private lives.
Every word sent out on social media, recorded and filed. Every step we took
in a downtown area, every purchase we made, every penny we had, all known
and recorded.*

*But that wasn't the part that caught my attention. It was how easily and
quickly people allowed it to happen. They were busy. They had nothing to
hide. They didn't have time to question it. Surveillance of the American people
as we had never seen before. And a level of public corruption that extended our
gradual acceptance of the absurdity, eventually resulting in the election of an*

unfit president lacking all of the prerequisites to be a leader. And many were okay with the corruption that accompanied his presidency.

The government seemed to have come unhinged from those it was supposed to serve—the people—and it seemed now to be run by some deeper entity that had one thing and one thing only in mind: World domination. Power. A slow rolling back of justice, equality, law, women's rights, family values, working values…and in their place an entertainer, distracting us from the pressing issue of climate change. This president was by no means the beginning of the problem, but he was proof that Americans were not so much concerned with their previously held, precious beliefs of family and honesty as they were with winning and power—or at least the perception of it.

Governments are subject to evolutionary changes, as is Nature. When something is out of balance, Nature finds a way to fix it if we don't.

THE HEADBOARD HAD BEEN HER GRANDMOTHER'S. Sharina had come from the Northeast Kingdom area of Vermont and was part of the Abenaki tribe, or what was left of it. Her mother was Abenaki and her father was Asian—"a very unlikely couple," her grandmother used to say. Her grandmother was all Native and lived on tribal land in Quebec. Sharina was always looking at her grandmother's dark complexion and straight, black hair and wondering what it must have been like to live among her people a thousand years ago. Not that Grandmother was a thousand years old. But her skin and hair were beginning to show the passing of time, and that made Sharina *see time*.

The headboard is solid maple, with scroll work from the 1950s. Sharina traces the wood grain with her index finger, making curlicue circles around the knots and along the currents of the wood, thinking how the grain resembles a river. *Her* river, where she was a child and would lie alongside the bank and allow her fingers to dangle in the cold waters that swirled around them.

She had met Paul just a year before, when she was finishing college. He was working on his PhD and was teaching software programming, a class Sharina would never take. At the time, she was a participant in the university's annual Indigenous People's ceremonial dinner, an event that the university sponsored to uphold its commitment to "equity and diversity." Sharina would perform ceremonial dances alongside various tribal descendants, mostly from the West. She was the only tribal woman from the East and the only Abenaki descendant that she knew of at the university.

She had met Paul when there was no place for him to sit and he had asked whether the chair next to her was taken. Dressed in her tribal outfit, she had looked up at him with her powerful, dark eyes. She had nodded her head, eyebrows raised, and turned away from him while he sat down.

Sharina pops up from the bed, her thoughts returning to the apartment they had shared for the past year.

"If you don't want me to come with you to California, just say so." Pulling a long piece of hair away from her face, she sits up tall and straight and looks at her boyfriend Paul.

"It's not that I don't want you to come, Sha." Paul continues throwing things into his suitcase, hastily preparing to leave for the airport. "I'll be working the whole time and I need to focus on delivering the best presentation possible to this client. It's such short notice and I don't want to mess this up. Besides, you've got work. Who would cover for you for three days?"

Sharina stops what she is doing. "Don't you dare use my job as the reason I'm not going." She grasps his shirt. "I hate it when you try to manipulate me like that." Her eyebrows raise, a sign that Paul has learned to read as *Listen up*. Releasing him, she swipes her robe off the chair on the way to the drapes and opens them to view the small, green park across the street with its brightly colored play structures.

The large maple tree outside their back window is a grounding ritual every morning. It was Sharina's "Mini morning meditation." "I love the way the sun creates layers through the leaves like childhood artwork." Sharina looks up at Paul and smiles, catching him glancing over her way. "It's like tissue paper with light shining through. Always reminds me of elementary school and the joy of art class." She stretches forward into an earth touch, followed by a sun salute in front of the window.

"Okay, then," Paul says. "Call a sub and let's go. We need to leave here in twenty minutes." Paul moves into the bathroom and grabs his shampoo and shaving bag. Stuffing his shaver into the bag, he looks at Sharina standing by the window, her length accentuated by the long draperies.

Slowly he walks back into the room. He tosses his bathroom bag into his suitcase and walks over to her. "I love you, Sha. Are you worried that I don't love you or that I can't be trusted?" Coming up behind her, he wraps his arms around her waist and pulls her into him, noting the stark contrast of her dark-colored torso against his light-colored arms.

"I just needed to hear that you want me to come," Sharina says.

Paul draws her closer and kisses her again. The quick kiss becomes more passionate as the two begin to move together. Paul pulls away. "I don't have time to do this right now. I've got to go," he says.

"You started it," Sharina replies with a playful shove.

Kissing her smooth, sweet-smelling forehead, Paul steps away to finish packing. "This is a huge client for us, and I'm really not as prepared as I'd like to be." Paul is a stickler for organization and planning. It's something Sharina remembered liking about him when she first met him. He had brought her a more expansive idea of organization, everything from lined-up towels on the top shelf of the closet to getting the oil changed in her car on time. But as the relationship moved on, it felt like an expectation he had of her as well, an unwanted expectation to always be on and working.

"You'll do fine, Paul. I'm sure you are plenty prepared. Trust yourself." She smiles again at Paul as she crosses in front of him.

"The guys in Silicon Valley are tough, and this particular company has a federal grant as well as private money to develop our new technology. That's a lot of people to please. Both groups must be accountable in order to keep the money coming in, so I need to convince them I'm the professional who can do that for them."

"Software companies are all the same," Sharina replies. She walks into the bathroom and begins to brush her hair out. "They want you to be God." Flopping her head over, she continues stroking her hair with the brush upside-down. "I'm sure if anyone can impress them, it's you." She throws her head back up, her black hair flying over her head and then relocating around her shoulders as she brushes back along her forehead line.

"I've got to go." Paul kisses her cheek and walks toward the apartment door. "I'll be back in three days, and you can call me anytime. I wrote down where I'm staying, by your phone. He stands at the open apartment door, looking back at her as she leans out of the bathroom doorway.

"You'll be brilliant. I'll call you tonight." Sharina walks over to Paul and hugs him, then calmly places her head on his chest. "Be safe in California. It's where all the weirdos live, you know?"

Paul embraces her warm head lightly against his chest, and Sharina can hear his voice from deep inside of him. "That's funny, I thought they all lived here in Portland." The two laugh as she squeezes his hand before releasing it.

"Bye, Sweetheart. Break a leg!" Sharina says.

Paul's tall shape begins walking away down the hall of their apartment building. "Bye," he says, turning back to look at Sharina. But she has already gone inside.

MORA LIKES WATCHING AARON while he sleeps. His blonde hair is at rest; his heavy arms are at rest; his agonized eyes are at rest; his soft, freckled face…finally resting. Looking across the bedroom at the early morning shadows forming, she realizes she is still in her work clothes. Carefully she rolls off the bed and peels away the layers of work. Reaching for her robe on the velour chair, she throws it around her and ties the tie, still watching Aaron sleep. As his chest rises and falls rhythmically with each breath, she flashes back to the night before.

"I'm home, Honey, you still awake?" Mora had shouted back toward the family room. She could feel a draft coming through, and it forced the front door closed with a slam when she released it. Setting her purse on the entryway table, she had slowly walked back to the kitchen to find the door open and Aaron pacing in the backyard. He was drinking beer and throwing the bottles at the back fence, scattering broken shards to fly across the dirt. "Aaron, what's going on?" Mora asked.

Aaron had turned back to look at Mora, his lovely wife. It was as if she were a mile away. She didn't belong here. The noise inside his head was loud, like the sound of tanks with their inter-twined metal treads, rolling, moving, in his head. And then the explosion hit and it was deafening as he dropped the bottle he was holding to cover his ears. The scream was from his guts, his innermost anger, like poison that had to be released. Dropping to his knees, he had started banging his head against the ground.

Mora had reached into her pocket for her phone and dialed 9-1-1. The welcomed voice, "Nine-one-one, what's your emergency," came back at her.

"My husband has just returned from Afghanistan and he's going crazy. Please send someone to help!"

"Do you need an ambulance? Is your husband conscious?"

"Yes, he's screaming! Can't you hear him?"

"What is your name?"

"I'm Mora Lambert. My husband, Aaron Lambert, has been home from his Afghanistan tour for two weeks and he's going crazy in the backyard!"

"Mora, I've sent help. Stay with me on the phone."

Mora had put the phone back in her pocket, still connected to the 9-1-1 operator, and stepped down the back porch steps toward her husband.

"Aaron, I've called for help. What can I do?" Slowly she had approached him.

"Don't touch me, I'm poisoned. They poisoned me. They said we were fighting for democracy, but it was all a lie. A huge fucking lie, Mora! Soldiers were crazy, hurting innocent people. I told them. I tried, Mora. But then they would hurt me if I didn't go along with it," Aaron had sobbed, rolling his head back, facing upward toward the stars. Then he cried loudly into the night air. The neighbor's spotlight outlined the waves of body heat coming off Aaron's back in the cool evening air.

"Are you still there?" Mora had asked into the phone.

"Yes, Mora. Have the police arrived yet?"

"Why did you send police?" Mora had cried. "We just need an ambulance. My husband is sick."

"The police can help keep him calm until the ambulance comes."

A knock on the front door had drawn Mora's attention away from the phone.

"We're back here," she had called toward the front yard.

A police officer had looked over the fence at the man weeping into the lawn and the woman crouching near him, with the phone in her hand.

"Officer Cole, Ma'am. What seems to be the problem? Does your husband have a weapon?"

"What?" Mora had looked at the young officer. "No, he doesn't even own a gun."

The officer then stepped into the yard and walked toward her. Suddenly, Aaron had raised up and screamed at him, "You LIED and now I'm like this. You LIED."

The police officer had looked at Mora.

"He just returned from Afghanistan two weeks ago," Mora had explained. "He's been having trouble."

The police officer then reached down for his two-way radio and called in to the main office, telling someone he needed backup.

"He's not going to hurt anyone. He's just upset," Mora had tried to explain.

Paramedics then arrived and opened the gate. As they approached the officer, the red lights from their vehicles were dancing around in the trees of the backyard as dusk began turning into night.

"Vet," was all the officer had to say to the paramedics. "Let's see if we can give him something to calm him down."

"Sir," the officer had said to Aaron as he moved slowly toward him. "Can we give you something to calm you down? It will help you relax."

Aaron's tear-soaked face had looked up to see Mora, scared, staring down at him.

"Aaron, I'm here," she had said, looking back into his fear. "I'm here, Sweetheart. Let these men help?"

"What? Where am I?" Aaron had looked truly bewildered and lost. His blonde hair was smeared across his face with some blood from a shard of glass that had shot off the back fence and stuck to his flesh.

"You're home, Aaron," Mora had replied soothingly. "You're having another attack. I called for help. I was afraid."

Aaron had looked at the officer and the paramedics. His mouth hung open, loose, as if his lower jaw wasn't attached. Then he closed it and sat back on his heels. "I'm sorry," he said, looking down at his hands. "I'm so sorry, Mora. I tried to stop it."

"Honey, it's okay. Just let these men help."

Aaron had then sat all the way down on the ground and looked up, nodding, depleted.

The two paramedics moved in and began to take his vitals. "Sir, we'd like to give you something to help you sleep. Is that okay?"

Aaron had nodded weakly as he exhaled in frustration. "No hospital!" he said as they inserted the needle. He looked up at Mora. "Promise me!? No hospital…"

Mora had looked down at her husband, whom she barely recognized. "I promise, Aaron. We'll just get you some rest. I won't let them take you anywhere."

As the medicine trickled into Aaron's vein, his eyes got heavy and he whispered again, "I'm so sorry. I'm so sorry, Mora."

"Please, help me get him into bed?" Mora had asked the paramedics.

"Ma'am, we really recommend you let us take him to the hospital and have him checked out there."

"What? No! He's had enough people lie to him. No hospital. I promised. Please, help me get him into his bed."

The two men had looked at each other. "You'll have to sign a refused transport waiver."

"Yes, that's fine." Mora had reached out for the pen that the other paramedic was handing her and signed the paper, pushing against the cold, metal clipboard box.

The officer had then helped gather Aaron, who weighs close to two hundred pounds, up from the ground. The paramedic grabbed under Aaron's other arm and they walked him toward the house. The strange men in Mora's house made her feel uncomfortable, even though they were helping.

"This way," she had said to them, opening doors toward the bedroom. She pushed things off the bed and onto the floor.

Slowly they had helped Aaron onto the bed. The paramedic checked his vitals again and then wrote something down. "Are you sure, Ma'am, you don't want us to take him?"

Mora interrupted, "I'm sure, yes. Thank you so much, all of you. Thank you. We can work this out. We just need some time." She had then herded the officer and paramedics toward the front door.

The officer reached into his pocket for a card. "I'm leaving my card with you, and you can call anytime if you two need some help. The VA is very good with PTSD cases and can help."

Mora had looked at the officer. "PTSD?"

"Yes, Ma'am. Many soldiers returning from Afghanistan have post-traumatic stress disorder. You're aware of what that means?"

Mora was tired. She had just come off a twelve-hour shift at the local ER, where she works as a front-office receptionist. "Yes, I know what that means."

***

From the quiet of the living room, Mora watches Aaron sleep the deep sleep of drugs, release, absence, freedom, rest. The officer's words from the night before burn at the front of her thoughts as she moves into the bathroom. "Many soldiers returning from Afghanistan have post-traumatic stress disorder. I'm leaving my card with you…" Aaron had been so excited about his enlistment to fight the evils that had come to New York, the airplanes, and the buildings. People jumping out the windows of the ninetieth floor, trying to escape the intense heat. He had believed he was going to punish those who brought this atrocity to America, his country. But his letters home from Afghanistan began to reveal a different purpose, one Aaron was fighting against, absent the supposed foe. She remembers the last letter she had received before they stopped coming. "They're killing women and children, Mora. Civilians! Everywhere there is chaos and I don't even know why I am here."

Then, three months later, he had arrived home. His two-year tour was over and he was home, broken, angry, fitful, and unable to rest.

Setting her toothbrush back in the available hole in the ceramic cup, she looks up into the image of herself in the mirror. She had aged since Aaron's return. Every day a worry. She closes her eyes and can see the night he'd made love to her, so passionately and with so much joy, and then, when they both climaxed, filled with the other's closeness, he began to cry, sob, and then uncontrollably yell into the pillow under her head.

Walking over to the bed, she lies down next to him and softly places her hand on the side of his hip. Tears run down her face and she can hear them fall onto the fitted sheet with a light *plop*. *What have we done?* she anxiously thinks to herself.

T HE FIRST WEEK OF CLASSES at the state university has students buzzing in every direction on bikes, skateboards, cars, and on foot. Everyone is excited and busy and in a hurry. Sharina compares in her mind the students' demeanor and dress of the first day with those of the middle of the term. Everyone looks so well-dressed, sharp, and important when they begin college, and so washed-out and exhausted by the middle of the first term, realizing their debt and the problematic first-job situation that would ultimately lead them down their career path. Sharina wishes she could just skip the first week and begin teaching the second week.

Walking past the front desk, she shows her ID to the overanimated, "I'm the friendliest girl you'd ever want to know" student worker, and they exchange smiles.

"Sha, what time are your classes this term?" one of her yoga students, who is also employed at the center, asks while walking by the front desk.

"Hello, Ellen." Sharina turns to smile at her student. "I'm teaching the four to five and five-fifteen to six-thirty slots. Is that going to work for you?"

"I'll make it work," Ellen says as she moves past and walks toward the women's locker room. "I love your class," she yells back over her shoulder.

The staff clock-in room has a security door. Sharina slides her ID over the scanner on the wall, and the door buzzes then clicks open. "Hello," she says to two other staff workers who are checking keys out of the key box. They smile and nod. "Is the key box working better this year?" Sharina's voice is flattened by the air-tightness of the room and makes her a little uncomfortable.

"Yes, I guess they had it repaired over break." The woman speaking is a student teacher at the recreational facility. She turns to Sharina. "Hi, I'm Natalie." She extends her hand. "I've heard all about your yoga class. I hope to have some open time so I can try it."

"I look forward to that," Sharina says with a smile, while shaking the woman's hand. "What are *you* teaching?"

"I'm teaching the Abs class this term. I think I'm in the room next to yours during your five p.m. class."

"Have fun with that. I'll come peek in to say hi." Sharina smiles at the student-teacher as she and her friend begin to leave the key room. The metal door opens with a buzz and closes with a hard click. Airtight room again.

The time clock is on a computer screen asking for ID and password. Sharina looks at her reflection in the computer screen. This is her fourth year teaching yoga at the university. Having worked her teaching times around her classes the last three years of college, it is a relief this year to only be teaching and be done with taking classes. The university had hired her to manage the other fitness instructors' schedules and teach her eight hours of classes a week. The job affords her and Paul free access to the state-of-the-art fitness center, pools, saunas, and café. Not a bad perk, Sharina muses as she tries again to fight back the feelings of uneasiness and anxiety. The room is tight and devoid of Nature and windows. She thinks back to last year's graduation. It had been uneventful. Yoga was what she loved, and to stay on and teach seemed like an okay move for right now. Being only nineteen at the time she graduated, she felt she needed a year to just slow down. Meeting Paul last year and moving in with him had all happened so suddenly.

She nods and smiles while collecting up her purse from the floor. She hits the metal plate that releases the door. It buzzes and begins to open. She turns sideways to step through it before it fully opens. She is in the spacious lobby, the door loudly clanging shut behind her.

P AUL BOARDS THE PLANE and surveys the seats. Slowly the line of people moves down the aisle, each locating the number on his or her boarding pass. Paul continues past people pushing bags into the overhead compartment and situating themselves in their seats. Seat 10C is occupied. Paul looks at his boarding pass again: "SEAT 10C."

"Excuse me, but I believe you're sitting in my seat," Paul says to the occupant of his seat.

A tall, dark woman with big teeth smiles up at him. She pulls her pass out to look at it again. "Oops, my mistake," she says, as she lifts her large body from the seat and moves one seat over toward the aisle. "There, I got it all warmed up for you," she chuckles.

Paul smiles. "Thank you, I appreciate that." He stuffs his bag into the overhead compartment while other passengers push past him and he moves his back out of their way while trying to shut the compartment. Ducking his head, he sits down in his seat and plugs his computer into the Internet dock. He feels confident about his presentation, but there are a few tweaks he wants to make before landing. Explaining the complicated workings of software to laypeople is always a huge challenge in his job, but it is often the most important part, since it gets his foot in the door.

"You going to California for pleasure?" the woman asks.

Paul's face is flushed and his large eyes deep blue, with lashes that extend outward to the corners of his eyes. He smiles at the woman. "No, all work this time. How about you?" Almost immediately after asking, he is sorry.

"I have three grandchildren I've never met before. My son is in the military and he just recently was moved to California from Germany, so now it's possible for me to see the kids. When they lived in Germany, it was just too far to travel. Not that I don't like traveling, because I do. It's just so expensive, and then there is the carbon footprint of flying to consider. I've never met my daughter-in-law and I'm a little nervous about our first meeting. She used to work for a hotel chain in Germany as a manager, but she left her job when the second baby came. The daycare costs, you know. They've become…" the woman's voice barely stops for a breath.

Paul nods and smiles, trying to be polite. His mind starts analyzing what makes some people think you want to hear their entire life story after just meeting. Sharina and Paul had both experienced this many times: A kind hello turning into a nonstop litany of one's life.

Paul interrupts the woman. "I'm sorry, I have to prepare for my meeting now. It's been nice talking to you. I hope all goes well with your visit." As he turns back to his computer screen, the woman continues.

"Oh, it will be okay. I'm sure the kids and I will find plenty to do, and my daughter-in-law is looking forward to someone taking care of them so she can get a break. It's hard being a mom these days with all the expectations on parents to begin educating their children before they even enter school. I was thinking maybe I'd take them..."

Paul nods and smiles while reading over his presentation. The flight attendant begins her safety spiel, dropping the life-saving device from above to be fastened over one's nose and mouth in the event of an emergency. Paul hurries to get through the first part of the presentation before having to put his computer away for the take off.

T HE UNIVERSITY RECREATION CENTER had been built in 2000. Before it was the state-of-the-art facility it is now, it had been a small, multi-room, brick building. Sharina remembers that building well. As a college freshman in 1998 she had taught aerobics in one of the small rooms. The massive wall of glass that runs along the second floor of the open mezzanine area makes Sharina reflect back on the modest beginnings of the center. Now there are a café and eating area, two Olympic-sized swimming pools, volleyball courts inside and out, ten full-sized basketball courts, and a climbing wall. When the place is busy, the noise can be all-encompassing.

The overhead fluorescent lights buzz while the TV downstairs can be heard playing sports network highlights over and over. Basketball sneakers squeak loudly off the gleaming courts below while cussing and yelling from the ongoing games echo upward. A plastic name plaque reading "MP3"—for Multipurpose Room 3—is on the heavy double doors. Sharina sits down outside the door, waiting for the previous class to end. She watches men, and a few women, working out in the weight room below her. She recognizes several young men who are regulars in the weight room. Their muscles bulge as they move from one set of weights to another. Sharina imagines herself going down and telling them that their muscles will do them no good as they age if they can't stretch them.

The double doors to the MP3 room finally open and students pour out, several waving at her as they pass. "Are you teaching the next hour?" a high, soft voice says as she rises to enter the room.

"Hello, Ana," Sharina smiles at one of her long-time students. "Yep, I'm in the five p.m. slot. You coming?"

The woman turns around and walks back into the room to chat with Sharina as she readies it for her yoga class. The room is large, with a wall of windows on the west side. This hour requires the shades to be down as the sun comes through at the end of the day. The floors were always in need of a quick brooming to sweep away all the debris of the previous classes. Then there were the lamps to be put in place so the overheads could be turned off, and the music selection needed to be up and running before the first students arrived.

"Hey, Ana, I need to run down to the maintenance room for a clean broom head. I'll be right back."

The young woman smiles and continues to scroll through the messages on her phone. Sharina is disappointed by how dependent on their phones some students appeared to be. They are constantly using them instead of talking to the people who are in their presence. *How do I teach them to be present when up against technology that encourages just the opposite?* Sharina would think to herself as she walked toward the maintenance room. "Hellos" and "How was your summer" come from several people she passes as she makes her way downstairs.

Opening the door to the maintenance closet, Sharina is surprised to find an older male inside. "Can I help you?" she offers, but he pushes past her. She thinks she hears him utter, "Fucking bitch," as he shuffles down the hall, away from her.

Looking inside the closet, Sharina notes that everything seems to be in place. "That's weird," she says out loud.

"What's weird?" a deep, low voice says from behind her. Sharina turns to find Trey Wilson standing there, all six-plus feet of him.

"A man was in here when I opened the closet and he practically knocked me down trying to get past me."

"They should keep the closets locked," Trey replies, and then asks, "How was your summer?"

Sharina smiles. "It was fine, Trey. How was yours?"

"We bought our first house!" he says, beaming with pride. "Boy, that's a nerve-wracking thing to do. It's a wonder anyone ever gets into a house, with all the inspections and paperwork and contingencies. Jenni has already sworn we will die in this house. She refuses to move again after this."

"I remember feeling that way the last time I moved. Can't blame her for that." Sharina looks through the different sizes of broom head covers lying on the shelf. Trey remains standing in the doorway. "Where did you guys buy your house?" Sharina asks him.

"It's way outside of town, in the southeast area. Not much to look at right now, but someday we'll have it all fixed up."

"That's so exciting, Trey! I'm happy for you guys. Your first house is a big step, but it sounds like you're both ready for it."

"Yeah, Jenni says she refuses to live in an apartment when the baby comes. Too noisy and too many weirdos. We're both real happy."

"And when is that baby due?" Sharina had forgotten that Trey was expecting soon.

"In four weeks. Jenn is counting the days down as she gets bigger and bigger."

"Do yourself a favor, Trey, and don't tell her that?"

"Oh, I know. Actually she looks really great for being eight months along. I've already learned what I can and can't say. You know Jenni. She doesn't let anyone get away with anything."

Sharina smiles, remembering her ex-student Jenni Wilson. "Got to go, Trey, excuse me. My class awaits."

Slowly Trey moves back from the closet doorway to let Sharina pass.

"Hey, have a good class," he hollers at her.

Walking back to her upstairs gym room, Sharina spots the man who had been in the closet, sitting at a table in the downstairs eating area. She looks his way and notices he is watching her as she makes her way up the stairs. He doesn't look like a student, but more like a man who works in a field. He is clean-shaven but is dressed in a baseball cap, camo jacket, jeans, and boots, and is wearing an old, green, heavy-duty backpack. His baseball cap is pulled down so Sharina can't quite see his eyes. At the top of the stairs she turns to see if he is still there, but the seat is empty.

"Hey, Sha, I'm so excited to be back in yoga class again," a voice says as Sharina moves into the lane of student traffic and toward her room. "Did you have a good summer?"

S IX SOFTWARE EXECUTIVES SIT around a large, oval table in the center of a glass-walled room. Paul moves in and out of the slides in his PowerPoint presentation, delivering his layperson's explanation of the software.

"So you believe you could have this up and running by the end of next month?" one of the men sitting at the table asks as Paul finishes up his presentation.

"I have it up and running now," Paul says. "I just need to work out a few bugs and maybe figure out a way to encrypt our back-door access for emergencies, but I could have that done in just a few weeks."

The five men and one woman look around the table at each other and smile. Kyle Christiansen, the owner of Axis Software, stands up and shakes Paul's hand. "That's great. Good presentation, Paul. We appreciate it."

Paul looks around at the others and smiles as the handshake continues.

Finally Christiansen lets go of Paul's hand and allows him to gather his materials. "We'll get back to you in a few days. Need to talk among ourselves and crunch a few numbers. You're looking for a downpayment upon delivery and a final payment after two months of bug-free operation, correct?"

Paul wasn't used to people being so upfront about the financial aspects of an arrangement during a presentation.

"Ah, yes, I think that is what we had agreed on in our previous exchange." Paul continues to place items in his bag while disconnecting his computer from the conference table port.

Everyone shuffles around the table to Paul's side and shakes his hand before exiting the room.

"We'll be in touch, then," Christiansen says before leaving.

Kyle Christiansen had started his company when he was just out of college. It had grown quickly. His willingness to bring young people on board had positioned the company as one of the few that could compete with the big boys.

Paul sits alone in the quiet room. He pulls his phone out of his shirt pocket and calls Sharina. Her phone rings and then goes to message. Paul looks down at his watch. Six-forty-five p.m. *She's not quite out of teaching yet.* So he texts her, "All went well. Look forward to seeing you tomorrow. I love you."

He slides the phone back into his pocket and flings his bag over his shoulder. The door to the conference room is heavy, and Paul has to lean into it to get it to fully open. Once in the hallway, he looks for an "EXIT" sign down both corridors and sees it to the right. He walks toward the sign, finds a bay of elevators, and punches the "Down" arrow. A door opens at the left end. Paul walks toward the opening elevator door. A young man gets off and looks at Paul. Their eyes meet and they smile.

"Paul! So *you're* my competition! I should've known." The man is well dressed, handsome, in his early twenties and just a few years younger than Paul. The two do a man hug, and as the other man,

Collin George, steps away from the elevator, he asks, "Where have you been hiding since college?"

Paul is surprised to run into one of his old college students. Collin was the only student at Cal Poly with whom Paul felt he'd had a meeting of the minds. Collin had been a student in Paul's programming classes.

"I hide out in Portland, Oregon, these days," Paul replies.

"Who would have thought our professor Stone would end up living in Portland with all the millennials?" The two men allow the elevator door to close as they stand talking just outside the bay.

"How about you? Anyone settle you down yet, or are you still doing bong binges and cheap beer runs?"

Collin smiles. "No bong binges for this old dude, and my beer tastes have moved more toward the microbrews, I'm afraid. It's a costly shift from cans to fancy restaurants with good microbrews. I'm not married, though, no. I've come close but it didn't happen. I live with my sister and her husband and my two nieces now, not too far from our stomping grounds near the university."

Paul ventures to ask what he really wants to know. "You here to pitch software?" Collin is the only person he knows in his circle of software geeks who could possibly come up with a better software program than Paul. But it had been a long time since Paul had seen any of Collin's work.

"Of course. But don't worry. I'm sure you're going to get this gig." Collin looks down at his watch. "I got a meeting in ten minutes. Let me give you my contact info and we can catch up." Collin puts his hand out for Paul's phone and enters his phone number into it. He hands it back to Paul with a smile. "Call me sometime?" His large hand pats Paul's shoulder.

"I will," Paul replies, checking Collin's contact number. "Maybe we can get you up to Oregon this summer to visit?"

"Summer might be possible," Collin says, smiling, as he moves toward the conference room. His step is large and confident.

Paul nods in his direction and then turns toward the elevator button and pushes it again. "Good luck," he says as Collin walks away, raising a hand to acknowledge the well wish.

The elevator door dings and opens. Paul steps inside. While heading down, he thinks back to Collin's final project at Cal Poly. Something about integrating biology into chips to make them faster and more flexible and increase their storage capacity. The project was way ahead of its time, and Collin's instructors had not been impressed. But later, when biological chips had become a reality, Paul remembered his student's idea and wondered if he had gotten in on the ground floor of that.

" **I** JUST THINK EVERYONE NEEDS a little garden space, a piece of land to connect them to their humanness. I see it, Paul, I see it every day. Young people with a completely lost look in their eyes, as if they are individual planets floating through the universe, untethered."

Paul's tie is still on but loosened as he makes his way over to the small kitchen table in their apartment. Their age difference of ten years is never more apparent to him than at the end of the day, when he feels exhausted and Sharina looks so beautiful and full of life. Tonight she looks particularly full of life, her face radiating as she looks up at him.

"What are we going to do with a house and land? We're gone all the time."

"Not all the time." Sharina still has her yoga clothes on and is tugging at a hair tie to release the long, braided rope of hair behind her. "Besides, I don't want to raise kids in an apartment."

Paul reaches for a glass in the cupboard and looks back at Sharina. "Then we'll get a house when we're ready to start a family."

He continues to pour himself beer from a large bottle, tilting the glass sideways to control the foamy head forming.

"When do you think that will be?" Sharina flicks her hair.

"When we both decide we are ready to make the sacrifices we need to make to raise a family. I don't think either of us are there yet, Sha. You just finished college and you did that early. You're just nineteen years old and we've only lived together for a year. I love you, but starting a family is a huge step, and…" he pauses. Looking at Sharina walk across the room toward him, he feels a twinge of hatred for himself. He has to tell her. *You're afraid you'll lose her*, he thinks to himself. *You have to tell her.*

Sharina looks back at Paul. He has pulled his tie all the way off and laid it over the back of the couch before sinking himself into the cushions and opening his computer in front of him. He looks out over the top of his beer glass to watch her make her way into the bathroom. Her silence warns him to tread carefully. Sharina was that way. When she talked and was vocal, he knew where he stood. But when she got quiet, he floundered and knew she wasn't happy.

Setting his beer down, he walks to the bathroom door, which is open a crack. He taps lightly on the door.

"You can come in," she says. Pushing the door open, he finds her sitting on the toilet, seat down, her pants pulled all the way up and her hands covering her face.

"I'm pregnant," she says, looking up into Paul's face.

S HARINA'S HANDS LIE QUIETLY in her lap as she sits, legs crossed, against the wall. The angry man paces in front of her and then turns and presses the gun up against her temple. The hard metal barrel pushes her head over to one side.

"You don't remember me, do you?" The man stares into Sharina's eyes as he releases the gun's pressure against her head.

Sharina shakes her head and whispers, "No."

The man resumes pacing. She recognizes him as the one who had been watching her a few days ago, from the downstairs café. But she doesn't know who he is.

"Two-thousand-one. We were in the jetted pool together, right here in this building. My commanding officer was sitting across from me, and you overheard me talking to him about killing Hezbollah."

Sharina nods. "I remember," she says, looking up into the angry man's blue-green eyes.

"Do you remember what you said to me?" The man bends down to get his face closer to Sharina's.

She shakes her head slightly and whispers again, "No."

"You said, 'Don't believe them,' and you motioned toward my commanding officer. You said the war was a ruse and that I could die if I followed this path. You said it would be very dangerous... do you remember that?"

She does remember the conversation in the spa pool. It had been two years ago, but she remembers it. "I remember," Sharina replies, looking up at the angry man. And then, conjuring every ounce of courage she has: "I'm glad you didn't die." She feels her fear dissipate.

"*What!?*" he yells at her in disbelief. "*What did you say?*"

"I said, I'm glad you didn't die." Sharina looks right into the man's eyes and sees confusion come into his face.

"Lady, I have a gun to your head, and you say you're glad I didn't die?" The man pulls the gun back and resumes pacing in front of Sharina. The wooden rec floor squeaks under the heaviness of his step.

Finally he stops pacing. "*I'm* not," he says. "I wish I had died. Do you know why?" He looks up again to meet her gaze.

Sharina shakes her head *No*, relieved he has removed the gun from her temple.

"So I wouldn't have to feel what it is to be me. I've killed innocent people—people who didn't want to die. I can't forget all the ugliness of being over there." The gunman waves his gun toward the east wall. "It was fucking *hell*," he says, moving away from Sharina, his head down. Muttering "Fucking hell" again, he slumps to the floor and begins to sob.

Sharina doesn't move from the seated position the man had forced her into. The man's sobs deepen and his shoulders begin to shake. "I'm sorry," she whispers toward him.

The room is silent for a moment except for the man's sobs. Then he looks up. His face is tear-soaked and he wipes his nose with his gun in hand. "Yeah? Well, that doesn't fix anything, does it?" he says, setting the gun down on his other side. "That doesn't fix a *fucking thing*," he mumbles, placing his head into his hands. "Why weren't you more persuasive? You should have stopped me from going. You were the only one who said anything about *my* well-being." The gunman turns his face toward Sharina's. He is a foot away. "Everyone wanted the bastards dead for what they did to us in New York. But you said it was dangerous and I might get hurt. Why? Why did you say that?"

Sharina can hear people outside the double doors of the room. She takes a deep breath. "I don't remember why I said it to you. You were so young, and I must've believed you were too young to know what you were doing, so I said that. I just didn't believe in that war. And I wasn't entirely sure Afghanistan nor Osama had anything to do with nine-eleven. Several other buildings also collapsed that day that had no planes hit them. Lots of things put doubt in my mind. What does going to another land and killing innocent people do but line the pockets of the war machine?"

The man's head rolls back into his hands. "Yeah, well, you were right. It *was* dangerous, and now I wish I were dead. I can't sleep at night and I keep seeing the faces of those people we killed. I didn't even know anyone who had died in the Twin Towers when I left for Afghanistan. I hadn't lost a single friend or relative, or even a pet up till then." The man laughs a little out his nose, then lifts his head. "Death isn't what you think, if you've never seen it before. It's dark and final and…" His voice stops, and he looks out the huge windows into the sun going down outside. "Forever."

Sharina hears someone outside the double doors, knocking lightly on one of the them. "I need to tell the students outside something," she says to the gunman, "or they will go downstairs and get staff."

The man looks up from his hands and motions with his head toward the door. Sharina gets up slowly, watching the man the whole time. "I'll just tell them I'm not quite ready for class. That will buy us a few minutes." The man watches her thin shape make its way over to the large doors. *Us…?* she had said. *How could she be on my side after I pulled a gun on her?*

Sharina pushes the door open a crack and is met with a group of young college students. "I'm sorry, guys, I'm not quite ready for class. Five more minutes?" Everyone backs away from the door and shuffles over to the benches to wait, pulling phones from pockets and talking to others.

Sharina shuts the door and walks back over to the man, who is slumping onto the floor.

"Here," the man says, looking up at Sharina and handing her his gun. "Don't worry, there aren't any bullets in it. It's not even my gun."

Sharina slowly takes the gun in her hand. "Can you show me that there are no bullets in this?" She holds the gun in front of him. Dropping the cartridge out of the gun, he pulls back the shaft to show that it's empty.

Sharina takes the gun and the empty cartridge from his hand and walks over to her bag, shoving them both inside, under her street clothes. "Come on," she says, turning back to the man. "We need to get you some help." She puts her arm around his shoulder and reaches her hand out in front of him.

"Lady, I think you should call the police. I brought a gun into your classroom."

She smiles at him. "Yes, you did. But I'm betting you have someone who loves you and who would come and get you. I think that is what's best. I'm going to put your phone number into my phone so we can stay connected. You can call me anytime, okay?"

The man twists his head sideways to peer through bangs that shield his eyes.

"You didn't listen to me last time—remember?" Sharina says. "Let's say you listen to me this time?" she smiles.

The man drops his head again into his chest and weeps. "Mora," he says as he hands Sharina his phone. "She's number one on speed dial. She'll come."

Sharina takes the phone from the man's hand and hits "1." A young woman's voice connects. "Hi, Sweetheart," the voice says. "What's happening in your world? You make it home yet?"

Sharina can tell the woman is moving around, believing she is speaking to her husband. "Hello, is this Mora?"

"What's wrong with Aaron?" she immediately replies to the stranger's voice on the other end.

***

Aaron and Sharina walk closely together through the double doors. Yoga students are waiting outside the doors, some looking down at the pool through the opposite side of the hall's windows, some on benches, some texting on their phones. They all look up as the doors open.

"Sorry, guys," Sharina smiles. "Go ahead and go on in. I just needed a little time to talk to my friend, here. I apologize for holding you up."

Everyone smiles back and begins collecting up their backpacks and belongings. Aaron keeps his head down. Several students glance at him, noticing that he's visibly upset.

"I'll be right back," Sharina tells them. "I'm going to see my friend to the front door. Ellen, you're in charge until I get back, okay?" Sharina catches Ellen's eyes as she comes toward her.

"Sure," Ellen says, briefly looking up from her phone. "No problem, Teach." She looks up again and smiles at the troubled man walking out of the room, next to Sharina. Ellen's gaze hesitates on the man's face as he ducks past, looking downward, passing between her and the open door frame. Sharina guides him toward the stairs.

"What kind of car does she drive?" Sharina asks Aaron.

Aaron's face turns up briefly at the question. "Light blue Subaru."

Sharina had told Mora to pull up in front. The two stand inside the building's foyer, waiting for Mora to arrive.

"You're going to be okay," Sharina says. "You just got scared and you probably want your life back the way it was before you left for Afghanistan." Aaron looks up toward her again as she continues, "It will never be the same. But it will get better. You have to have faith and move forward. And Aaron," she pauses and looks deeply into his face. "You have to get some help. You and Mora cannot do this on your own."

Dropping his head, he bounces it in agreement. "I know...I don't know why you're helping me, but I do know that I will forever be grateful for this."

The light blue Subaru pulls up in front, with a young woman driving. She gets out and heads for the double doors of the recreation center.

"Hi, I'm Sharina." The two women look at each other while students hustle around them, standing in the building's quad entrance. The sun is hot, beaming off the concrete as it sets behind the west hills.

"Mora," the woman says, placing her hand on her chest, over her heart. "I can't thank you enough."

"No need for thanks, but Aaron and I had a little talk and he's promised that he will go get some help." Sharina looks at Aaron, who is ready to head to the car. He turns back and grabs Sharina's hand.

"Thank you, Sharina. I am going to listen to you this time." A small smile crosses his face as he wraps his arm around his wife. "And keep the gun. I never want to hold a gun again."

The two head off to their car. Sharina walks over to the side parking lot and places her bag into the trunk of her car. Slamming the trunk closed, Sharina notices the beautiful sunset beginning in the west. *I've tried to save him twice now*, she muses as she returns to the rec center to teach her yoga class.

PAUL KNOWS HE HAS TO MOVE, but his hand is glued to the bathroom door frame. He can see that Sharina's face is happy but scared.

"Sha, that's amazing!" he says, trying to move from the bathroom door. "That's great!" he tries again.

"Come on, Paul. 'That's great' and 'That's amazing' is the best you can do?" Paul looks stunned. Sharina watches him as he steps backward into the room and sits down on the couch. She slowly walks into the living room and stands in front of him. "I know we're young, Paul, and I know we've only been together for a year, but it feels inevitable to me. We've been diligently practicing safe sex and I am pregnant. It feels right to me, but it's wrong if you're not in it with me. I love you, Paul. I want to have this baby."

Paul feels the soft couch cushion's inability to support his body's weight. Deeper he sinks into the couch, unable to move.

"*Say* something, Paul!" Sharina sits down on the coffee table in front of him.

Paul reaches out and takes her beautiful brown hands in his and pulls her closer.

"Sharina, there's something I need to tell you."

Sharina's eyebrows raise and she leans toward Paul, squeezing his hands lightly.

"Sha, I can't have children. I'm sterile. Completely sterile. I know it was wrong of me not to tell you, but we had been together such a short time. It didn't seem like something either of us were considering right now in our lives, and I knew if we eventually decided to have children, we would figure something out."

"*What?*" Sharina's mouth drops open and she pulls her hands away from Paul's. "*No!* she shouts, shaking her head, "that's impossible. I'm *pregnant*, Paul, and I haven't been with anyone but you. You *have* to be wrong about that. Evidently whoever told you that you were sterile was wrong, because here we are and I'm at least six weeks pregnant."

"Sha, I had a vasectomy. I decided a long time ago that I didn't want to contribute to an already overpopulated planet. Seven billion people is enough, and it just seems like all the problems of the world circle back around to human overpopulation and overconsumption. There is no way the child could be mine unless my vasectomy failed in some way. I'm sorry. Now I wish I had told you when we first met. It just never felt like the right time. I'm so sorry."

Sharina's mouth hangs open as she pulls further away. Then she shakes her head slowly. She stands up and reseats herself next to Paul on the couch. "No, no, no, *no!* I'm telling you, Paul, I haven't been with anyone else. Just *you*. Only you. If I'm pregnant, this is your baby."

The two sit on the couch in the silence of their confusion, with only the background noise of traffic holding the room together.

Finally, Sharina speaks: "We'll go to a doctor and see what they have to say. There must be tests that'll prove it's yours." She gets up and moves into the bedroom. She shuts the door firmly, leaving Paul sitting on the couch, alone.

"Damn it!" he says out loud into the empty room.

THE ABENAKI PEOPLE WERE Natives of Vermont, New Hampshire, Quebec, and other regions of the area known as the Northeast Kingdom. Sharina's mother is part of the Nulhegan Abenaki. She lives just outside the town of Barton, Vermont, where Sharina was raised. Sharina remembers the pasture lands that surrounded her home and the gently sloping hills that seemed to cup her home like hands. She was small-community schooled growing up and resented the feeling of being cut off from "the real world," as she had told her mother. When she finished high school at the age of fifteen, she emptied her savings account, kept in a ceramic pig she'd been stuffing since she was nine years old. Summers of berry picking and working on local farms had made "Piggy" sufficiently full.

"The old ways are not for me, Mom!" Sharina had said shortly before leaving home. The argument had taken place several times while she was growing up. "I need to go to a real school, with real people, and then maybe I'll return after I finish college."

Sharina's mom had agreed that school was a good thing, but she didn't want her daughter forgetting her love for the land, and the importance of tribal connection and her history, "as told through our people…" her mother would say with a sigh and her brows drawn down over her eyes. Her mother was young, having had Sharina at age eighteen. When Sharina asked about her father, her mother would say he had done all he could do just creating her. "He wasn't family man material," her mother would finish. Her mouth would close and her head would shake and she would look away from her daughter. End of conversation.

"Mom, I'll be taking some classes about the Tribes' history," Sharina had tried to reassure her. "I'm aware of the preciousness of storytelling and the tradition of oral passing down of knowledge. You don't need to worry."

"Mothers must worry in a world of so little love for Our Mother." It was her mom's favorite saying, referring to Mother Earth, an entity she worshiped. Sharina often wondered if her mother was depressed to the point of being ill. But then they would have a conversation about their people's history, and Sharina could see the truth in it for her mother and sense in her the destruction of her tribe's people, the complete loss of their land, their children, their traditions, and all they held sacred and loved. It was serious.

Listening to her mother's stories when she was little, Sharina would sit in wonder with her eyes growing bigger. She remembers how the stories would sometimes frighten her and thought it mean of her mother to tell them to her. She would feel the sorrow and heaviness of her mother's facial features, and she resented her for that. As she grew older, that heaviness was something she had to work through.

"I love you, Mom. I'll call tomorrow…" she had shouted back over her shoulder as she got on the bus for a ride to Burlington's International Airport, where she would board a plane for Portland, Oregon.

And she had called her mom the very next day, after meeting her roommate and getting their room together. "See, Mom, I'm still right here. We can talk any time." Sometimes the conversations felt superficial to Sharina, but she could feel her mother through the phone. The conversations meant everything to her, even if they just talked about the weather. It was good to have her mother right there. At just fifteen, she was young to be going to college. Having finished high school early, Sharina was excited about being with other young people, hearing about where they came from, and learning about things that were happening in the world. Special arrangements had been made for her at the university, and eventually she had been admitted and was allowed to live on campus. Her scholarship had made it financially possible, and she wasn't going to waste her opportunity. But she'd be lying to say she wasn't really looking forward to the social side of school as well.

Freshman year, she had tested out of all her prerequisite courses. Being an avid reader, she found the entry-level classes a waste of her time. The second-year classes challenged her and she worked hard to do well.

Feeling lost in the dating scene, she had joined the Indigenous Peoples Meeting Group, and by late fall she had participated in her first meeting with others from tribes all over the U.S. But most of the students were from indigenous tribes of the West, likely because of their proximity to the university. The other students talked about growing up in their communities and the stories their family members had passed down.

Sharina had sat in the circle meetings and listened. Her tribe was different from Western ones. Her tribe was still fighting to gain federal recognition, something that would help her people financially but that had not yet been secured. Many of the Western tribe students were receiving money from the government that made it possible for them to attend school.

By contrast, Sharina's income came from her scholarship and her part-time job teaching yoga on campus in the evenings. The pay was good, though, and it gave Sharina a way to meet other students without dating, something she hated doing. By her senior year in college, she had been elected leader of the Indigenous Peoples' meetings and had spearheaded a night of entertainment to bring in money and help support their longhouse meeting place on campus.

***

"These are beautiful, Mom," Sharina had said as she took out the lovely, handmaid ceremonial dresses her mother had wrapped up, in a box, under her bed. The dresses were brightly colored around the neck and waist and wrists. They were heavy and yet comfortable. Sharina had tried on one of the dresses and immediately felt at home, standing in front of the large mirror in her mother's room. "Are you sure it's okay for me to borrow these, Mom? I know they mean so much to you."

Her mother had nodded and smiled. "I'm proud of you, and that you are going to dance for everyone at your college in my dresses."

Sharina was to perform the Jingle Dress Ceremonial Healing dance at the event. With the dress on, standing in front of her mother's dresser mirror, Sharina had felt something strange happen inside her. It was like movement, or a warming that welled up from her genital area and exited out the top of her head. She reached for her mother's dresser to hold on.

"Are you okay?" her mother had asked, leaning in toward Sharina.

"Yes, I just feel so strange and tingly. I'm fine. I'll take this off now and go get a drink of water." Sharina had then carefully laid each dress back into the right box and covered it with the sheet her mother had wrapped them in.

"You could come to the ceremonial dance and watch, Mom. It is a long way to travel, though, and I understand if you can't."

Sharina's mother had replied that she would pay to have the dresses shipped to Oregon but "can't afford" to come out. But Sharina knew her mother would never fly on an airplane. Flying was "against Nature," as her mother had characterized it. Sharina had long since given up arguing on this point.

The visit back to Vermont had been short this time, but Sharina and her mother had met up with two other tribal women from Sharina's childhood, Minki and Lisa, to have lunch. Both women had farms near her mother's. They wanted to hear what was going on in the West, where Sharina was studying. Sitting around the large café table, they had all shot questions at her: "Do you have a boyfriend yet?" "Are the people pushy and rude out west?" "What's your favorite class?" "What dance are you going to perform?"

The questions had kept coming throughout the meal as Sharina tried to eat her sandwich and not talk with her mouth full. But she loved the women who were her mother's friends. They were strong women who had been very present in her growing-up years. Sharina could not remember any part of her life without these two women in it. They worked their farms next to her mother's farm, each one focusing on a different crop. They called her mother by name, which always made Sharina see her mother with different eyes.

"Teylen, you must be so proud," Minki had said to Sharina's mom. "Sha is in college and bringing our ways to many people. She is a light."

Teylen had nodded and smiled while Sharina tried not to laugh, so as to be respectful toward her elders, her mom's friends. Head down, she had resumed trying to make progress on her mostly uneaten sandwich.

Later that day, at home, Sharina had prepared for the trip back to Oregon. She looked out the small window in her old bedroom at the brightly colored leaves that hung in autumn's pause. The wind challenged their tenacious grip on the branch until one fluttered down, touching ground, being still.

Sharina loved her bedroom but felt a little overgrown, returning to it after two years of college. The stay had been for just a week, but it was the right amount of time. She was ready to return to school and classes.

Hugging her mother at the shuttle pickup spot in town, Sharina didn't let go.

Teylen felt her holding on and continued to embrace her. "You are brave and strong and we love you. Everyone here loves you," she had said.

Sharina knew what her mom had meant by "everyone"...all her mother's friends and the animals that dwelt on the land with her mother.

"I know, Ma. I love you, too. I had just forgotten how much love I have for this place, until I came back. It holds a big part of my heart." Sharina had then released her mom and stepped back. "I'll miss you."

"But you'll call me as soon as you get to the school, so I know you are safe from the flight?"

"Yes, Mom, I will call."

They had hugged one more time, and then Sharina stepped up onto the bottom stair of the shuttle.

"Watch for the dresses to arrive," her mom had called out. "It will take about ten days from when I mail them, tomorrow."

"Thank you, Mom, for doing that. I will watch for them."

The women had smiled at each other, and then Sharina was gone.

Teylen could feel the loss that is part of motherhood. To grow this life inside your own body, to have it be a part of your biology, feeding it with your food, through your blood, inside your skin in a Mother Ocean where it dwells like a fish for most of a year. Then to release it through birth, into the world of air-breathing, and to protect and love and nurture it for so long. This was the reward of motherhood. The joy of growing life and protecting and teaching and sharing in one's child becoming a person. Nothing could have prepared Teylen for the loss she was experiencing with Sharina leaving home, just like nothing could have prepared her for the love she had felt when she was born.

"I'll be coming back," her daughter had said. But Teylen knew that Sharina would never come back again to be her daughter in the way she had been. The second umbilical cord was being cut, and Teylen felt it, deep in her soul.

"I'll be waiting for you here," Teylen had said as the shuttle drove away. Then she turned and walked home, alone.

ORA AND AARON SIT in the waiting room at the office of Dr. Joshua Connor, psychiatrist, waiting for someone to call their names.

"Mr. and Mrs. Lambert?" the receptionist nods toward them. "Come this way, please." They walk the hallway of the V.A. hospital and enter the doctor's office.

"Come in, please," Dr. Connor says as he motions them to the couch. He walks toward them and stretches out his hand. Aaron takes the hand and shakes it firmly while looking deep into the psychiatrist's eyes. Mora reaches forward and lightly shakes his hand. The two sit on the couch, Mora repositioning to accommodate placement of her purse.

"So, Aaron, you are a returned vet?"

"That's right," Aaron nods, leaning forward, forearms resting on his spread legs.

"And you're angry and having flashbacks? Am I understanding you correctly from your intake questionnaire?"

Aaron smiles and thinks for a moment before answering. "Yes, I'm angry, Doctor. I'm angry because no one told me the truth about Afghanistan. I felt lied to." Aaron stretches his head forward and clears his throat.

Mora watches the doctor.

"Who lied to you, Aaron? The government, the army, your platoon sergeant?"

Aaron doesn't like the doctor's tone. He and Mora had argued before making this appointment. "I think we should see a doctor who isn't part of the military," Mora had said. "Someone who won't get in trouble if they agree that you were lied to."

"We can't afford that, Mora," Aaron had replied. "The V.A. only covers the doctors inside their network. We have to see one of these. We just don't have the money to see someone at two-hundred dollars an hour outside of that network."

"But we want answers and not more lies, and if you go see someone inside the network, they can't really talk to you about Afghanistan in a way that would make sense to us. They have to side with the military and the military's mission." Mora was adamant, but Aaron only saw dollar signs because he wasn't bringing in any money now. And that was what hurt most of all.

***

The counseling session over, Mora and Aaron sit in their light-blue Subaru in the parking lot, staring out the windshield, silent. Finally Aaron speaks up: "I feel even madder than when we went in."

Mora reaches across the seat to Aaron's arm and rests her hand on it. "We'll figure this out. We need to get to someone who isn't inside the military, Aaron."

Mora straightens up, starts the engine and begins driving toward home. She switches on the CD player and navigates to the playlist she had compiled for when the situation called for calming music. Aaron turns his head away from her and looks out the passenger window. Hot tears of rage flow down his face. There seems to be no end to the tears, no end to the rage.

THE LAB AT TWENTY-SIXTH AND MORRISON is undetectable from the outside of the building. There isn't any signage. People walk by it every day, unsuspecting of what goes on inside, like so many other buildings in cities. It is just a building, accepted by the community and unquestioned.

"I've never seen anything like this." The lab researcher places her laptop down on her colleague's desk. "The young woman is not intersexed, and yet her lab tests come back saying that she is."

"What about her male partner? What showed up in his tests?" her colleague asks.

"Her companion is shooting blanks. He was right about that. There is no chance the baby is his." The woman pauses and continues looking at the blood readout. "But at the same time, there is no chance of our understanding the baby in any terms other than the mother's biology, with these tests looking this way. It's impossible. I've never seen anything like it before."

Dr. Carol Porter stands up and looks at her fellow researcher. "If I were trying to understand the results of these tests, I'd say the mother is also the father. How can that be?"

The two look at each other.

Porter continues out loud, as if in review of what she knew to be scientifically true. "The most extreme signs of sexual development disorders are those known as 'sex inversions': 'XY' women with undeveloped testicles, as well as a vagina and a clitoris, and 'XX' men with testicles and a penis. In all recorded cases, these people are sterile. There are many other intermediate phenotypes in which both male and female sexual characteristics coexist in the same individual."

While mulling this over, Dr. Porter moves to the other side of her colleague. "Thus, XX babies with congenital adrenal hyperplasia are born with female reproductive organs and masculinized external genitalia. But this young woman tests to be an XX and displays female in and out. She swears this man is the only man she has ever had sex with and that he is the father, and yet it's impossible. When I look at the mother's test, something is very different. It's unreasonable to place the two biological sexes present in the vast majority of people, on the same level as the extremely rare intermediate sexes. Yet this woman falls into an even rarer category, one I've never encountered before. She isn't intermediate in her sex. She shows as a female, and her chromosomes test as a female."

Muttering to herself, Dr. Porter heads back to her office to make a phone call. Her colleague looks back over his shoulder and watches her walk down the hall. He sees her not quite close her office door. Then he peeks at the name on the test: "Sharina Mathews, Portland, OR." There is also a phone number. The assistant writes the information down and closes his computer. Walking back to Dr. Porter's office, he peeks through the slightly opened door.

"I know, Peter, but I'm telling you, the woman is asexual, if we are to go by what the tests say." The man lightly taps on her open door. "Just a minute, Peter," she says into the phone as she turns to look toward the door.

"I'm heading out, Carol, unless you need me for something else," her colleague says to her.

Dr. Porter looks up at the clock on her wall: six o'clock. "I'm sorry for keeping you so late," she replies. "Yes, go. Have a good weekend, Huang." She turns around to finish her phone conversation.

Huang Li walks down the hall to his desk. He opens the file, takes out his phone, and snaps a picture of the young woman's file. He closes the file and walks out.

"I HAVE NEVER LOVED ANYONE BUT YOU, Paul," Sharina says for the hundredth time. The test results haven't come back yet and the interim has the couple stewing in the incomprehensible. Sharina knows she has only been with Paul, no one else, and Paul is equally certain that he is completely sterile. They are stuck.

"Look, Sharina. You're young and you committed to me young. I will completely understand if you wanted to be with a few other people in your life. We can talk about this and be truthful."

Sharina's face turns a deep crimson under her pinkish brown skin. She feels crazy. *Why are the tests taking so long to be returned!?* "No, Paul. I love you. There is no one else. I don't want there to be anyone else." She hops off the barstool where she has been sitting in their dining room and grabs up her yoga bag. When she lifts it, it feels heavier than usual.

The gun. She hadn't told Paul anything about the incident with Aaron and Mora. Paul had been so preoccupied with the software program he was hoping to deliver and get paid for, finally. The years of subtle abuse growing up Native in a white culture had made Sharina able to understand people on a very deep level.

There had been no real threat with Aaron. He was just trying to connect up the dots in his life so he could get back to where it was working for him. Sharina could tell he was a good person, the same way she could tell something big was coming her way. She felt it in her cells. Her mother had taught her to listen to and value the knowing that came to her.

"I have to go to class, Paul. I love *you* and *only you*," she says as she moves to the front door of their apartment. "I teach all day today. Please, let's go out for a peaceful dinner tonight and just be us? I need some time of no stress so I can think." She stands in the doorway, waiting for a response from Paul.

He looks up at her and sighs. "Sure, Sha. I love you, too. No matter what. I'll make a reservation and text you." They pass the energy of love across the room toward each other, both equally confused by the situation but willing to stay together.

After Sharina shuts the door, Paul looks out the huge windows on the east side of their apartment building. He does love her. It's truly the only thing he is certain of in his life. Even if they were not together, he wouldn't want any harm to ever come to Sharina. She had brought a light into his life that he didn't know he had lost. He always felt calm and whole when she was around him.

Turning to his computer, Paul opens his email. *There it is…*the email he'd been waiting for from Axis Software.

Then his phone rings. He doesn't recognize the number, but the name on the screen is clear: *Kyle Christensen*. "Hello, Kyle. I just noticed an email from Axis. I'm hoping it's good news."

MORA AND AARON'S DAYS ARE PASSING in a holding pattern. Mora gets up from bed and hugs her husband. "Time to get up," she encourages. She heads off to the shower, and Aaron sits on the side of the bed with his head in his hands. The drugs make him useless in practically every way. But their lives are restarting, and the chaos of the PTSD has taken a backseat to the commitment they both have to bring life back together after Afghanistan. "There has to be life after your tour with the military," Mora would tell Aaron. "It's going to take time, and we should use whatever tools we have to buy us that time." She was encouraging him to take the anti-depressants and get some sleep.

And sleep came like an anvil falling on Aaron's head. At first he slept straight through for thirty hours. Mora woke him and forced him to drink water and use the bathroom, but he would just fall right back into bed and sleep another twenty-four hours. She would come home from work and find him exactly where she had left him twelve hours earlier. Sometimes she would just fall asleep next to him, unable to do anything else after her long shifts at the hospital.

One morning, though, Aaron was up before Mora and had made breakfast.

"What's all this?" Mora had asked, coming into the kitchen and motioning toward the poached eggs, toast, and coffee.

Aaron's smile was something she hadn't seen in a while. He had continued smiling at her. "It's breakfast for my hard-working wife."

Mora had stood in shock at her husband's loving gesture. She smiled but then was unable to hold back the tears. They exploded from her eyes and she covered her face.

Aaron had walked around the kitchen bar and embraced her. "It's going to be okay," he told her, even though he didn't believe it himself.

Today he forces himself off the side of the bed and into the kitchen. Pouring both of them a bowl of granola, he gets out two spoons and cuts up a banana on top of the cereal. Mora comes out from the bathroom, all dressed and ready for work. The two smile at each other and sit down at the small kitchen table. No one dares speak. The sound of Afghanistan is too loud between them, and any extra noise may bring back the PTSD. The cereal is lifted to their mouths and they chew.

"You're going to keep getting rest today, right?" Mora says after a long silence. It was hard for Aaron to let go of being Mora's protector and the family breadwinner. But this is the path that life was laying out for him, and rest seems to be the thing that is making him better. Every day, he writes in his journal about his experiences in Afghanistan. He doesn't let Mora read it, but it does make him feel better to get it out.

"Yes, I'll rest, loving wife." He smiles and takes her hand. "What did I do to deserve such a good wife?" he asks while kissing her fingers lightly.

"My! You are in a good mood today. But still rest, right?"

Aaron nods and returns to his cereal with a boyish grin.

The small house feels foreign to Aaron after Mora leaves. He moves about the kitchen and cleans up after their quick breakfast. Walking over to his phone, he texts to a familiar number: *Things are getting better and Mora and I are always grateful for you. How are things with Paul? We're both here for you if you need us.* He sends it. The two had been using each other as a backstop during their life challenges, and the texts had become a part of their days.

Paul still thinks it's not his baby, reads the reply. *Staying busy and trying not to think about it right now. Glad to hear things are getting better. I'm here for you as well.* Sharina had been hesitant the first time she received a text from Aaron. She had written to see how he and Mora were doing and whether he had secured a counselor. The conversation had just never stopped, and the two had become each other's support system.

Have a good day, Aaron texts. *Take a break from the worry for awhile.*

Sharina reads the text and has to laugh. *Look at you, texting out encouragement and sunshine* [three smiley faces].

Aaron laughs out loud when he receives her text.

Sharina leaves her yoga bag in the back seat of her car and heads into the recreation center. One of her students catches up with her and walks with her toward the entrance, chattering about…something.

Just as they reach the large, concrete area in front, Sharina notices a woman and a man staring at her. Sharina looks toward her student's ebullient face as she speaks, then looks back at the two people. They are definitely staring at her. Sharina places her hand on her student's arm. "Ellen, would you mind starting class today?"

Ellen smiles at her friend and teacher. "Sure thing, Sha! Are you feeling okay?" She places a hand on Sharina's cheek, faux-checking her temperature.

"Yes, I'm fine. I just need to talk to those people over there." Sharina nods toward the couple.

Ellen looks in the direction Sharina nodded and sees the two people waiting for something. But then she catches them both watching her and Sharina.

"Is everything okay, Sharina? Who are they?" Ellen squints as she tries to bring the couple into focus.

"I'm not sure, but I'm going to find out." Sharina turns to Ellen. "Don't worry, it's not a big deal. I'll be in soon. Thank you for starting class today."

"No problem," Ellen says, as she lets go of Sharina's arm and walks toward the rec center's large, heavy glass doors.

Sharina turns toward the two people and walks up to them. "Can I help you with something?" she says as she comes within earshot.

The two look startled that she has called them out, but the woman quickly finds her composure and begins to talk. "Are you Sharina Mathews?" she asks.

"Who's asking?" Sharina looks at the woman's large briefcase and the tall Asian man sitting next to her.

"I'd like to give you my card, in case you need some help with your lab results when you get them." The woman hands Sharina a card with information on it. "Just email me if you want someone to talk to."

Sharina takes the card and looks at it. *Dr. Carol Porter*, it reads. *Lab Biologist, Tom McCall Medical Building, Portland, OR.* And it includes an email address and phone number.

"I'm confused." Sharina eyes the woman's outfit and the man next to her. He looks kind—definitely not a threat. "Why are you privy to my lab work? Why isn't my doctor's office calling me?"

"They probably will soon. Just keep the card in case you need to call, okay?" With that, the woman and the man walk toward the parking structure, leaving Sharina standing in front of the rec center, holding the card, dumbfounded.

Reaching for her phone, Sharina calls her doctor's office but is immediately put on hold. "Of course!" she says. Giving up for now, she makes her way up to her yoga class to relieve Ellen.

PAUL IS ALREADY HOME when Sharina opens the front door. He had texted her shortly after she left for work, saying he wanted to have a dinner at home and could they go out another night? He'd cook. Sharina loved Paul's cooking, so she had replied, *No problem*. He had set a fancy table with candlesticks and flowers, even though he knew Sharina didn't really go for that kind of thing.

"Hello, and what's the big occasion?" Sharina places her things down in the hallway, and then hugs Paul.

"I've got great news." Paul's face lights up. He is more excited than Sharina had ever seen him before. "I'm it! You are looking at the new software developer for Axis Software!" Paul turns slowly in front of Sharina as if something about him has suddenly become miraculous.

Sharina smiles. "That's great, Paul!" She hugs him again, but this time their eyes meet.

"That's great? Wow, now I know how you felt when I said that to you in the bathroom."

Sharina smiles, remembering. "I'm sorry, Paul. I just had a really weird day today. Congratulations! I'm so proud of you, and I'm not surprised at all."

The two make their way to the kitchen, where Paul opens a small bottle of wine and pours one glass. Sharina turns on the kitchen faucet and washes her hands in the sink.

Motioning to the empty dining chair, Paul says, "Come sit here and tell me what was weird about your day." He sets his wine glass down at his place and pulls her chair out.

Sharina sits down. "We weren't going to talk about the pregnancy, and the weird thing has to do with the pregnancy."

Paul immediately looks worried. "Are you okay? Is the baby okay? What happened? I don't care if you talk about the pregnancy. What happened?"

Sharina undoes her long braid and lets her hair relax around her. She draws her legs up under her and sits cross-legged in her chair. "A woman and a man met me outside work to hand me this…" Pulling the card out of her side pocket, she places it on the table, close enough to Paul that he can read it: *Dr. Carol Porter.*

"A doctor?" Paul pulls back, perplexed. "And it isn't *your* doctor. What did she want?"

"I'm guessing she was from the lab that did our blood work." Sharina pauses and sips her water. "She had brought a man with her, and on her briefcase it said, 'OHSU Lab Services.' I tried to call our doctor but I was put on hold, and it probably would have taken fifteen minutes for anyone to answer, so I hung up." Sharina picks up her water again and drinks down the whole glass. "What's for dinner? I'm starved!"

"I don't like it, Sha. Someone is following you?" Paul walks over to the large stew pot and dishes up beef stew, heavy on the vegetables, the way Sharina likes it.

"Ah, stew! You *do* love me." Placing her napkin on her lap, she immediately begins eating. Pausing between bites, she says, "I need to call my doctor and find out what's going on. Tomorrow, though. I'm tired and need to eat and rest."

Paul sits down and sips his wine. He takes a few bites of stew before replying. "It bothers me, Sha. I think you should avoid your workplace until you find out what the doctor says and why these people came there."

"We'll see," she says with her mouth full and smiling. She holds her water glass up in the air. "To Paul's success," she says.

Paul hesitantly holds up his glass and clinks hers. They both smile.

T
EYLEN WANTS TO CALL SHARINA but keeps telling herself not to bother her. The pull toward the phone to make the call won't release her, so she finally calls, dialing the landline phone in hopes of reaching Sharina's cell phone. When Sharina's voice message says to leave a number, Teylen hangs up. "Drat!" she says to the empty kitchen in her small house.

Walking to the back door, she grabs her coat. She steps outside and slides each foot into a farm boot, then walks over to the chicken hut with her basket. The chickens follow her to the hut as the evening sun begins to sink below the hills.

"Come on, girls, time to settle in for the night." The chickens gather around Teylen's legs and one by one make the small jump into the coop. Inside, Teylen has to duck to avoid bumping her head. The chickens all fly up onto the sleeping board. The requisite amount of pecking-order jostling takes place before they settle down.

"Red, you know that is Queenie's spot. Move down." The large red hen moves over one spot, allowing Queenie to flap up into her place. "Thank you, Red." Teylen checks the nests for a few straggler eggs and then shuts the nest boxes down. She has rigged the nest box door to open automatically when the coop door opens in the morning. Keeping the hens out of the boxes at night means less cleanup.

Teylen loves her chickens. She hums them a song while she checks their water and straightens a few things inside. She fingers each chicken lovingly on their breast feathers and talks to them in a low voice. "Everyone get a good night's sleep. Thank you for the lovely eggs, and I'll see you in the morning."

The chickens have a look of deep contentment on their faces as they settle in for the night.

Teylen looks out over the fields that roll green all the way to the hills in the distance. The setting sun creates a lavender color close to the ground that increases in intensity as it moves upward, toward the starlit evening sky. Taking a deep breath, Teylen stands and watches. She can hear the hoot-owl in her friend's barn, and a reply from the quarry hollow up the old, dirt road.

Another breath. Coyotes skitter across the fields, looking Teylen's way. She picks up a stick and cracks it loudly over her knee. The coyotes run off, yipping and communicating to their fellow travelers.

Heading back inside, Teylen removes her boots on the edge of the concrete porch and sets them in the boot tray just inside the mudroom door. It is fall, her favorite time of year. *Why do I feel so antsy?* She walks over to the phone and picks it up again, but hangs up before dialing.

She sits down in the kitchen chair, picks up the TV remote, and angrily clicks it on. Pensively she reaches for her smoke box and takes out her pipe and a small jar. She unscrews the jar lid and takes out a small amount of bud.

After a few puffs from her pipe, she clicks the TV off. *What is making me so anxious? Something* was happening, but she couldn't see it clearly…yet.

She goes back to the phone and picks it up. Pressing Sharina's number into the buttons, she decides to go through with it this time.

"Hi, Mom. What's up?" Sharina's voice sounds happy but tired, coming from across the country.

"Do you feel something coming?" Teylen says.

"I know, Mom. I do."

"Remember to listen, Rina." Her mom hadn't called her 'Rina' in years. It was a loving term she used when she wanted to feel close. "And pay attention."

"I am, Ma. No worries. I'll call you tomorrow if I have a clearer picture."

"Remember to trust what you're feeling."

"I will, Ma. I promise. Did you tuck the chickens in yet?"

Paul is sitting next to Sharina on the couch, and Teylen can hear him chuckling at the conversation. "I did. We'll talk soon. I love you, Rina."

Teylen hangs up the phone and looks around her small home that feels so empty with Sharina gone. She walks over to the cat lying in the comfy chair and sits down, replacing him on her lap. "We miss our girl, don't we, Mr. Biscuit?" Teylen had given the cat that name when he started showing up on their back porch and Sharina would put out a buttered biscuit for him. He would eat it completely and go away until the next day. One particularly cold morning, Sharina had invited him in, against her mother's rules, and the cat had been in ever since. "She's a sly one, our Rina, isn't she, Mr. Biscuit?" Teylen holds the cat up to her face and nuzzles him.

H UANG LI HAD WORKED AT the McCall Laboratory Building for two years. His work with Dr. Carol Porter had allowed him time to do the research that interested him most—gender and genetics. His extended family lived back East, where they had relocated after leaving Taiwan. His wife and his young daughter were everything to him, but it was the work that had brought him here, to Oregon. He had relocated his immediate family near the lab, and his daughter Chana attended the local high school.

Huang's mother-in-law also lived in the house, and Huang was thankful for her helpful presence. "A house full of women is a wonderful thing," he had once told one of his coworkers. His daughter Chana had been unexpected, and Huang's wife was very young when she became pregnant.

When they were dating, Huang and June had talked briefly about having a family, and they had agreed that if they ever wanted children they would adopt. "Too many children already here with no love," June had said.

Huang had read about Dr. Porter's work studying atypical gender, and it had fascinated him. He had applied for the researcher job for that very reason. He loved his daughter Chana with all his heart, but he knew he couldn't have fathered her. It had become apparent to Huang as Chana grew that she was an extremely bright and engaged person. He resented the stereotype that Asians are always smart, but his daughter had become something of a wonder to him.

June had been eighteen when she told Huang she was pregnant. They had been dating only three months. Huang had never told June he was born intersexed, and although he was now biologically male, his chromosomes told a different story, having an extra X to his XY. He was also sterile. Thus, Chana had been a huge surprise, and although Huang didn't question his young wife, he suspected she had been with someone else.

"I love you so much," June would say to Huang in the evening, embracing him from behind and turning him around to kiss him lightly. He would look over at baby Chana sleeping on the makeshift bed they had created and feel the warmth of their home. He just didn't care how Chana had come about. *June loves me*, he had told himself. That was all he cared about. And he loved that child. She belonged to his heart and he knew it.

T HE NEW LAB REPORT STOPS HUANG dead in his tracks. A young, asexual woman. A woman having a baby independently of a man—*a parthenogenic birth*. Dr. Porter was right. It was impossible. But it would explain so much. And this woman is also of Asian descent.

Huang takes his copy of the report home to look it over. Chana is eighteen now, and is only home when on vacation from school. She has a life beyond them. Huang pores over the doctor's notes and the lab results. There has to be a clear, scientific rationale for what is going on with this woman, Sharina Mathews. Huang couldn't help but compare her with his wife June, and her pregnancy. *June was probably just too embarrassed or ashamed to admit she had been with someone else*, he thinks to himself. Two women turning up having the same rare ability? And in the same geographic location? They would have to be connected if it's true. *Perhaps after one of our brief break-ups, June had just gone out and been with someone?*

Huang continues looking over the lab results and having this conversation in his mind. The science of the report fascinates him and he can't wait to be home, alone, to give it a good going over.

***

June is sitting on the front stoop when Huang drives in to their driveway. He parks the car and walks up to where she is sitting. "Hello," she says first, as he comes around the row of shrubs that line the walkway.

"Well," Huang says, a bit put off, "you're home early."

June smiles up at her husband. "Yes, they let me go for good behavior. What's your excuse?"

Huang looks at his watch. "It's six-thirty, that's my excuse."

June looks at Huang's watch as he outstretches his arm. "Wow, where did the time go? Feels like I just came out here a few minutes ago, but it's been forty-five minutes." June moves over to invite Huang to sit on the step next to her. Huang was thinking she was going to still be at work, and he really wants to go inside and study the lab report. But he sits down and takes a moment. He kisses her lightly on her cheek.

She smiles at him. "Shhhh," she says, even though Huang isn't speaking. The two sit listening to the wind and the sounds of far-off traffic. "Hear that?" she asks her husband.

"No," Huang replies, "I don't hear anything but cars."

"Exactly!" June says, lifting her pointer finger gently in an upward motion. "I say it's time we move to where we don't hear cars when we sit in our front yard."

Huang smiles. It is a good idea, but not one he is ready to tackle this evening.

"I'll think about it," he says, hugging her lightly. "I really need to go in and look over something I brought home from work."

"What's that you say!?" June shoots back at him with a wry smile. "I don't think so! Isn't it enough that we've given our eight hours today, and now we have some time to just relax and perhaps have a meal?"

Huang knows he isn't going to get to look at the report tonight. He acquiesces. "I'm going inside to wash up. You coming?"

"I'll be in pretty soon," June replies. "You go ahead. We're having chicken, noodles, and veggies for dinner. Feel free to start cooking in there…"

Huang goes inside, sets his computer down, and heads for the bathroom. *Chicken, noodles, and veggies sound very good*, he muses.

THE HOSPITAL WHERE MORA WORKS is part of Oregon Health Sciences University. Her admit list is long today, so she sits for a moment to enjoy the coffee she purchased on her way in. Aaron was doing better. She smiles and takes a sip.

The sex had been a surprise. She'd awakened to his face right next to hers in bed. "Want to fool around?" he'd said, raising his eyebrows twice quickly, like when they first met. He lightly kissed her on her nose and then worked his way down to her nightgown.

"Don't you want to let me go clean up first?" she'd asked.

"No, I like you just the way you are." Aaron's head had popped up from under the covers. "Me and Mr. Rogers," he'd said, with a big grin.

Mora laughed. She hadn't laughed in so long that the sound of her laugh had caught her off guard.

Aaron then slipped his head back under the covers.

Afterwards, they'd showered together, and Aaron had made Mora breakfast while she got ready for work. On her way out the door, he had called after her in a sing-song voice: "Would you be mine, could you be mine, won't you be my neighbor?"

"See you tonight," she had said as she backed out the front door, smiling.

It was like a miracle, the way Aaron was improving. And Mora was beginning to feel different, too. Happier. Healthier. She thought back to when she had started feeling better and realized it was the day she had picked Aaron up from the rec center and met Sharina.

Taking another sip of her coffee, Mora flips through the files in queue for admittance. A Thomas Barker is coming in for gall bladder removal. A Sonya Cole is coming in for fetal ultrasound.

She continues looking through the files while sipping her coffee and reminiscing about Aaron's morning surprise. Then her coffee cup stops midway to her mouth.

Sharina Mathews, blood work, the next file reads.

Mora opens the file and looks deeper. On the surface it appears to describe the need for extensive blood work to determine paternity, but underneath it looks more complicated than that.

Peering through the transparent walls of her office, Mora sees that no one is around. Quickly she texts Aaron: *Did you know that Sharina is expecting and doesn't know if Paul is the baby's father? Due in for test today.*

She waits a moment. Nothing back.

Mora realizes that she may be in breach of doctor-patient confidentiality here, but she and Aaron had become friends with Sharina, and Sharina had told them about Paul. When she spoke of him, he was the only man in her life.

Why hadn't she said anything about the pregnancy? She couldn't be too far along, since Mora had seen her just a month ago when she came out of the rec center.

Bling… the sound of an incoming text turns Mora's attention back to her phone. It's a short message from Aaron: *Yes. Tell you about it later?*

Mora lets the phone rest on her chest. She peers out of her fishbowl office to see if anyone is around. Then she picks up her phone and texts back: *No. Tell me about it now, please?*

After a brief pause, her phone rings. Picking it up, she asks Aaron, "How did *you* know, but *I* didn't know?" She knew that Sharina and Aaron had become close friends after the rec center ordeal, and Mora hadn't minded because he had seemed so much better since then. They both had. "Is it yours?" she asks quickly, before she can really think the thought.

"No!" Aaron nearly shouts. "Why would you think I would be with someone other than you, Mora? You're my wife and I love you."

"I don't know. It just came out. You and Sharina are texting all day long, it seems."

"She helped me. And now I'm just helping her. Can we talk about this when you get home?"

Mora looks up to see co-workers passing by her office. "Yes, you're right. That's best. But I want you to tell me *everything* when I get home. Promise?"

"I promise. Are you still smiling from this morning?"

Mora feels herself blush. "Yes. Are you?"

"I'll see you tonight and I'll tell you everything. I love you." Aaron is just about to hang up when Mora's voice comes back at him.

"I'm sorry, Aaron. I'm sorry I asked you if you were the father. It's just been so hard since your return, and a lot of the time I'm on shaky ground."

"You don't need to apologize, Mora. I'll see you tonight. Bye." Aaron hangs up, and then texts Sharina: *Are you getting blood work today at OHSU? Is everything okay?*

I T's PAUL's DAY OFF and he leans back on the couch in their apartment, thinking. Paul had been on the job for Axis Software for several weeks when he realized his work was being compartmentalized, part of something bigger. That wouldn't have bothered him, except that he had been led to believe it was a singular project. He is debating whether to take this to his boss or sit on it for a while. Why would Axis Software need this indepth programming for magnetic energy processing? Axis wasn't an energy firm, and it was clear to Paul that his programming was being used for this purpose.

He taps his fingers on the top edge of his laptop. A bubble text comes up in his message program. It's Collin George. *Hey Paul. Christensen told me you landed the job with Axis. Congratulations. I need to talk with you and get advice on something, but in person. I'm in Portland, can we meet up?*

Paul is curious and excited about reconnecting with his favorite ex-student. *McMenamins, Tenth Street, thirty minutes?* Paul replies. He waits.

Great! Collin texts back.

Paul closes his laptop, wondering what this is about. Recently his mind had been focused primarily on Sharina's pregnancy, and the more he thought on it, the more excited he was about making a family. His greatest concern is Sharina's age and the fact that they had known each other only a year. But every night when she came home from yoga teaching, she would sit with him and they would talk about such things as her upbringing in Barton, Vermont, her mother and her grandmother, and the tribal women who were her mother's friends. They both would share stories of their lives, gradually intertwining them into a braid of one life between them.

The paternity tests had been inconclusive, and Sharina was to return for further tests, but Paul was finding himself not caring whether it was his offspring. He loved Sharina, and there was no ignoring it. It had been such a surprise that he had fallen in love at all, as love wasn't something he had believed in. But this was different from any experience he had ever had with a woman, and now he couldn't imagine his life without her.

Paul looks at his watch. Grabbing up his coat, he makes his way over to the door and closes it behind him. McMenamins is only a short walk away. *I wonder what Collin wants to talk about*, Paul ponders. He doesn't notice the man outside his apartment, watching him as he steps onto the sidewalk.

Mora's grandfather had served in Vietnam, and she often spent time at his nearby gravesite. Since Aaron's return, she felt conflicted about the military, and she wanted to talk to her grandfather, so she made the short drive to his gravesite. She brought a small broom and a rag to clean it up.

After sweeping the flat memorial marker, she rubs the rag over her grandfather's name—Captain Kenneth Peterson. His relatives had been second-generation Swedes. She would often just start talking when she came here to clean the headstone. "I'm not sure, Grandfather, how I'm going to be strong enough for Aaron. He seems so broken." Tears begin to fall as she continues. "I need a miracle to get me through this, and I want to be strong like you and make you proud of me." She had brought a bit of cleaning solvent diluted in water, which she sprayed on the marker and then rubbed clean. "I love him so much, Grandpa."

Mora's mind fills with the first time she met her husband. The store was busy but starting to empty of evening shoppers. She needed to buy a new television and didn't want to spend lots of time figuring out all the gadgetry on the popular new tech-heavy

TVs. She had stood in front of the long row of display screens, looking through the information offered on each. "I don't know," she had murmured under her breath.

"It's confusing once you start looking at all the specs." The voice had come from behind her, and she had turned to find a very attractive man, about her age, smiling at her.

"Yes, it would be easier for me if they came in some nice colors. Then I could just make my choice that way."

The man had laughed. "Well, I recently bought a smaller version of this one, and I'm very happy with it. But…" He had motioned her toward the end of the row of displays and started walking in that direction. "…I think this one over here is a better deal this week, made by the same company but with a slightly larger screen." He had smiled at Mora as she followed him to the TV he was pointing toward.

All the TVs had the same show on. It was *Mr. Rogers' Neighborhood*, and Mr. Rogers was singing, "Would you be mine, could you be mine, won't you be my neighbor?" as he took off his shoes and smiled into the camera.

"I love this guy," Aaron had said to Mora. "Sometimes I catch parts of his show when I'm at my brother's house and his kids have it on. Public Broadcasting is all he lets them watch."

Mora had watched the man's face as he spoke. His mouth moved in a crooked sort of way, and his smile came at her with the force of a warm summer day.

"I'm Aaron, by the way," he'd said. And then that smile.

"Oh, yes…Mora…Mora Peterson," she'd said, grabbing for the silver heart she wore around her neck and fiddling with it. Catching herself staring, she continued, "So you think this is a good set?"

"For the price, it's the best one here. And the warranty is fantastic." That smile again. "So, Mora, do you live around here?"

A shopper then bumped into Mora's back, forcing her to step forward.

"Uh, yes. I work at OHSU and live close by. How about you, Aaron? Do you live in Portland?"

"Well, for now I do. I'm being sent out on my first tour to Afghanistan in a few months, and then I'm not sure where I'll be stationed."

The two had continued talking about TVs and TV shows and where they grew up. Mora felt she just couldn't get enough of him.

"Would you go have lunch with me out in the plaza tomorrow?" Aaron had asked as he walked the TV out to her car. "I really like that place inside the little yoga studio that serves hot bowls of spicy beans and rice with veggies. Have you eaten there before?"

Mora wouldn't have cared if they served wet rags and potato peels; she knew she was going to lunch with Aaron the next day.

"Sounds great!" she'd said, scooting in behind the steering wheel. "I know the place. I've actually taken yoga there before." She'd smiled up at him, and the sun outlined his blondish red hair as he squatted down to be at her face level. "Ah, fantastic! I'm really looking forward to it. I wish it was tomorrow!"

Mora laughed. "Me, too." Her cheeks had started heating up. *Jesus God, am I blushing?* She hated that her quick blushing gave away her feelings.

"Well, all right then, Mora Peterson. I'll see you tomorrow at one at the yoga studio in the plaza. Oh, here's my digits in case something comes up or you get lost." He opened his phone and showed her the number. Mora had quickly punched the numbers in on her phone. She couldn't stop smiling. She had been smiling for so long her cheeks were starting to hurt.

"And don't forget," Aaron said after she started up the car. "I like you just the way you are."

Mora looked puzzled.

"Mr. Rogers…on the TV, in the store," Aaron explained, pointing at the department store.

"Oh, right," Mora answered back. "It's a beautiful day in the neighborhood…" she said, smiling.

"Now you've got it," Aaron said as he stepped away from her car.

Mora smiled and waved at him as she drove off.

You're going to marry that man was all she could think, even though she had purposefully avoided marriage up to this point in her life. She had a nice apartment and loved her job at the hospital. She appreciated the simplicity, but she had to admit, it was often lonely on a long weekend when it was rainy and cold out. "And that smile…" she had said aloud as she drove, then laughed once through her nose and shook her head. Pulling into her underground parking structure, she was already pondering what she was going to wear to lunch the next day.

McMENAMINS IS OPEN, but with few people inside at this hour. Paul walks through the door and looks for Collin. The dining room wraps around a large bar, so Paul moves toward the back of the restaurant to see if Collin has arrived yet. In the very back booth, a man in a baseball cap pops up and waves at Paul. Paul doesn't recognize him at first, but then he sees the familiar face under the cap.

"Hey! Good to see you, Collin. I didn't recognize you with that baseball cap on." Paul comes closer and shakes Collin's hand. He notices dark circles under Collin's eyes.

Paul sits down in the booth across from Collin and sees that he also has a slight, rhythmic tic, like the beating of a heart, in the soft area under his left eye. "So, what's going on at the DOD? That's where you landed, isn't it?"

"Thanks for coming, Paul. Yes, that's where I landed. A pretty good job, too, and I was super excited at first, but now I don't know." Collin looks around as if someone else is coming.

"Are you expecting someone else?" Paul asks, as he spreads himself out more fully in the booth.

"No, sorry. I've just become a little paranoid recently."

"Paranoid?" Paul sits back and looks at his friend. "That doesn't sound like you at all. What's up? How have you been?"

The waitress comes over and Paul waves her off.

"It's the programs, Paul, at the DOD. I realized last month that I'm working on something I'm not familiar with, so I started to dig a little deeper and find out what the whole was, beyond the part that I was working on. You know, the bigger picture? After a few questions and some research on the work computer, I received a very strong warning to back off."

"How strong? What was the warning?"

"My cat." Collin looks down as if he is going to cry. Very unlike the macho, funny man Paul knew.

"Your cat? I'm sorry, Collin, I'm not following you."

Collin looks up at Paul and then peers around the restaurant. "They killed my cat, Paul. As a warning."

"Who killed your cat? Who is warning you?"

"I don't know who specifically, but it's coming from high up at the DOD, I suspect. I also received an MYOB email, if you get my drift."

Paul was familiar with MYOB emails from working on sensitive projects for other companies. Accidental curiosity sometimes would elicit such an email. Usually a brief apology and explanation put the matter to rest.

"And then the next day I did some research from my home computer, and I think they're watching me at home, too," Collin says.

Paul hates seeing his favorite student so undone. "Come on, Collin. It can't be that bad. Are you still living with your brother and his wife and kids?"

"No, I had to move out. It put them too much at risk, and the government office space was too far of a drive. So I moved closer."

Collin takes off his hat, runs his fingers through his hair, and replaces the cap, pulling it down over his eyes. He clasps his hands, sets them on the table, and looks down at them.

"Okay, first, what do you think you're working on? What's the bigger picture, you know, the whole of the project, if you were to guess?" Paul reaches out and touches Collin's arm. He wants his friend to know he is there for him.

Collin looks across at Paul. "Some kind of huge weapon that uses microwaves to disassemble large objects. I've never seen anything like it. I've worked with the military before, but this is very different. I keep being reminded how top secret my work is, and then the cat thing just put a whole new layer on it." Collin looks down. "I think they're watching me all the time, Paul."

"But why? Why watch you?"

Collin shifts and sits up in his seat. "Nine-eleven, Paul."

Paul looks blankly back at Collin. "The towers?"

"Yes, think about it. What could bring buildings down like that and turn them into dust, the way we saw happen? And not be hot? People were walking around on the debris very shortly after the buildings came down. It should've been hot, and the paper in all those offices should've burned, but it didn't. Cars flipped over. And the more I read about the findings, the more I realized it had to be something other than just planes."

Paul is uncomfortable. He doesn't recognize this person who is acting so paranoid. It isn't the same Collin he thought he knew. "Well, what about the planes we saw fly into the buildings, Collin?"

Collin shrugs. "I know you think I sound like a conspiracy theorist. I know how crazy I sound, Paul. You think I like it? I hate sounding this way. It's not me. But I have looked deeply into the software being produced by some of my colleagues, and we are without a doubt perfecting some type of weaponry that 'dustifies' whatever it targets. Imagine the power in crumbling a whole city with magnetic vibrational pull. Maybe what we witnessed on nine-eleven was some kind of a test? Some type of dark-cover, underground weapons test that the Feds agreed to look the other way from and then blame it on the Afghanis supposedly harboring this guy, Osama bin Laden. It would allow Bush to go have his coveted war and keep the war machine happy. And then there are the buildings that came down without any planes flying into them. How is that so easily overlooked? I know it all sounds crazy, but there are others, serious scientists, who have done a lot of research on the facts of that day, and they also conclude that something we are not familiar with happened to those buildings. Their work just isn't popular."

Paul sits back and lets it sink in. He looks up at Collin and rubs his chin. "Then what were the planes about, Collin? I know we saw planes, and people's loved ones died. You don't want to sound like you're making things up in the face of all that loss. You have to be sure."

"Well, maybe the planes' fuel was needed as an accelerant, or maybe a vibration was needed to initiate the sequence? Or perhaps they were just a distraction, to create a cover story and allow the war to proceed? I don't know. I'm not saying I know. I'm just saying it's getting really weird and I'm noticing people watching me and following me. I'm getting nervous."

"It's okay, Collin. I'm listening. I hear you. You're not alone in this, okay?" Paul tries to get his friend to look him in the eye.

"You know that company you're working for has a big fat contract with the DOD?" Collin says, looking directly at Paul.

Paul's eyebrows arch and his mouth twists. "No...I wasn't aware of that. How do you know that?"

"That's how I got this job, Paul. Your boss, Christiansen. He personally walked me over to the DOD and put my hand in theirs. What does *that* tell you?"

This point really catches Paul's attention. Suddenly he remembers his recent feelings that he was being compartmentalized with his work, unable to see the full project, just being aware of the part he was working on. "That is interesting," Paul says, sitting back.

The two are silent for a while. Then Paul looks up at his friend and colleague. "Hey, did I tell you I'm going to be a dad?" Paul smiles.

"Wow, Paul. That's incredible news!" Finally Collin's face softens a little and he smiles. Paul can see the old Collin—briefly. Then Collin adds, "Now you *really* need to be careful, if your work is part of this!"

Paul hates that Collin has said this but realizes he is right.

The two talk a little more about possible fatherhood and the implications of their work, then they agree this will be their meeting spot, to reconnect in two days. "If you need to reach me before that or any other time," Paul offers, "just put a piece of masking tape on the front of the blue USPS mailbox outside my apartment. The mailbox is right there. I'll check it every time I come or go. That way we aren't leaving any trail for what could come later. When I see the tape, I'll meet you here. Write a suggested time on it and that's when we'll meet."

Collin starts to look a little better just as they are preparing to depart.

"By the way, what did happen to your cat?" Paul asks as they head for the door.

"Can't," Collin says. "I can't say it. It was bad. Suffice it to say that he's dead and placed on my front porch in a DOD hazmat bag." Collin opens the restaurant door for Paul and they both step outside. The sound of whizzing traffic is in the air. "I loved that cat," Collin says loudly, shaking his head. "He was the best cat, and he'd kept me company for years."

"Collin, I'm so sorry about the loss. Remember our meetup in two days and the signal for an emergency. I'm sure we'll both laugh about our paranoia when we figure this out. Maybe someone at work just had it in for your cat because you crossed some line you didn't know about? I don't know. I'm here, though. We'll figure it out."

The two man-hug before heading off in opposite directions.

The whole way home, Paul can't help wondering whether Collin is right. It would explain so much about why he keeps meeting with brick walls of resistance at work when he asks questions. His flights into Silicon Valley were weekly but brief. The company had no problem with him working from home, as long as he made the occasional trip in to the meetings in California. The meetings were not helpful, though, and Paul was beginning to think they were intended to disrupt his stride, introduce chaos. Christensen was always checking on whether the job was giving him any trouble, and to remind Paul to only work on the company's computer since it had the encrypted software needed to keep his work confidential. Paul was surprised other engineers were not meeting with him in California to go over the work. But Christiansen had wanted it this way, and until now, Paul hadn't questioned it. *Could I be putting Sharina and the baby at risk?*

Arriving at his apartment building, Paul looks across the street to see a large man standing there, leaning against his car, looking at the building's front door. Paul makes eye contact and waves at the guy. The guy looks annoyed and turns the other way.

"Hey," Paul yells at the guy across the street, through the traffic noise.

The guy looks back and shakes his head, as if to say, "What?"

Paul crosses through the traffic carefully and approaches within a few feet of the man. "What are you looking at?" Paul asks.

"Well, not that it's any of your business, but I'm waiting for my sister to come out of that building." The guy points to Paul's building.

"Oh, I'm sorry. I didn't mean to hassle you. I'm Paul." He extends his hand.

The man reaches out hesitantly and shakes Paul's hand. "Jim," he offers. "Jim Samuels."

"Again, my apologies," Paul says. "Just been kind of on edge with the break-in that happened next door. Did you hear about that?"

Jim shakes his head and makes a downward movement with his mouth. "Nope, I didn't."

"Your sister didn't tell you about the break-in?" Paul asks. "Who is your sister?"

"Oh, uh, Sheila Samuels. She didn't say anything about that." The man eyes Paul. "I'll have to ask her about it." The guy throws his half-smoked cigarette down and twists it into the pavement with his shoe. Paul notices several other butts of the same brand.

"Well, okay. Sorry again to come on so strong," Paul says. He makes a mental note to check for a Sheila Samuels in his building.

"Hey, I understand," the guy says. "I'm glad someone is keeping an eye on things." He shields his eyes with his hand to cut the glare as he looks at Paul.

Paul picks his way carefully back through the traffic to the other side of the street, where he turns around to wave at the guy. "Jim" waves back. As Paul's eyes move downward, they accidentally land on Jim's license plate: "U.S. GOVERNMENT FOR OFFICIAL USE ONLY." He nearly trips on the front porch step as he reaches for his apartment's door.

"**W**HAT ARE YOU UP TO, Ma?" Sharina is sitting on her couch as she speaks on the phone with Teylen in Vermont.

"Minki and Lisa are here, and we're just sitting around, having tea and talking about the old days." Minki and Lisa are like family to both herself and her mother. They are Teylen's best friends, who live down the road from her small farm. They had helped to raise Sharina.

"Say 'Hi' to Minki and Lisa from me? Do you want me to call you later?" Sharina can hear the women moving about Mom's kitchen and talking in the background.

"Something is wrong," her mother says. "I can feel it. What's wrong?"

Sharina can tell her mother has moved into another room.

"I need to talk to you, Ma. Can I call you later, after Minki and Lisa leave?"

"Talk to me now," Teylen insists. "What's going on?"

Sharina gazes out the large windows on the east side of her apartment. The day is sunny but threatening to cloud over from the west. It's smoky out today from the wildfires, some of them as far away as British Columbia. She moves toward the windows and sees Paul talking to some guy across the street, leaning up against a car. The man is pointing at their building.

"I'm pregnant, Ma." Sharina fiddles with the draperies, waiting for Teylen's voice to return to her ear. She lifts her leg into crane pose and places her foot on the inside of her other leg. "Mom?" She can hear her mother speaking with her friends in the background, then returning to the phone.

"You need to come home." Teylen sounds almost panicked.

"I don't know, Mom. Right now I need to stay here and work and figure things out with Paul. I'd love to come home and see you, though. It's just not a good time."

"I need to talk to you, Rina. How is Paul taking the news?"

"It's a long story there, Ma. He loves me, but…"

"But what?" Teylen presses.

"But he says it can't be his, and I know it *is* his. I haven't been with anyone else. So we went to get tests run, but evidently it was too early in the pregnancy to tell. The doctor asked me to come by the hospital for different tests." Sharina starts to cry a little. "I know it will be okay, Ma. I'm just a little scared and confused."

"Sha." Her mother's voice is firm. "The baby is special. Paul isn't the father. You need to come home. I will explain when you come home. We can't do this on the phone."

"Of course the baby is special, Mom, but what do you mean Paul isn't the father? I swear to you, Ma, he is." Sharina wipes away a tear that has run down her face.

"Sha, you need to come home *now*. I can't talk on the phone. If you need money for the trip, I will send it to you. Please?" Teylen never pleads or begs. Something is wrong.

Sharina stands on both feet. "Paul's coming up the stairs, Ma. I'll call you back after we talk."

"Sha, I mean it. You need to come home. I can't help you there."

Help me? Sharina ponders. "Okay, Ma. Let me call you back in a little bit. I love you."

"Sha, please listen to me. This baby is special. You need to be here, not there."

"Ma, I have to go. I hear you. Let me talk to Paul and I'll call you back."

Teylen hangs up the phone. She turns to Minki and Lisa, who are sitting at the table in her kitchen. "She's pregnant."

All three women get very quiet. Minki and Lisa move closer to Teylen. She is embraced by them and she feels their love. The three women move outside and stand in Teylen's front yard and remove their shoes. They stand in a circle and hold hands and say a prayer together. A prayer to the Universe to watch over Sharina and her baby.

"Dear Mother of all Life who brings miracles upon us daily. Let the way be safe for our Sharina, our daughter, and her child. Watch over her and keep her safe. Let wisdom grow inside her to bring her home where she is safe." The women start singing a song as clouds from the west move in overhead. They stand connected in a small circle among the rolling green pastures that surround Teylen's farm, and sing.

H UANG AND JUNE LI have a Saturday morning ritual of
visiting the farmers' market in Portland. Today, June's
mother, Luani, is joining them, and Chana has decided
to also come along. It is absolutely gorgeous out—cool, clear, and
sunny—the kind of morning that makes Portlanders walk around
with smiles on their faces. November brings in good produce, especially as climate change has created a longer growing season in
the West.

Huang had sat up for hours the past several nights, going over
the lab results. His boss, Dr. Porter, seemed satisfied that she had
made contact with the young woman and felt she had done all she
could to warn her without alarming her. The lab had returned to
its normal pace, and Huang appreciated that it was Saturday and
he didn't have to go in to work.

"This is probably the last week we can get produce before
we get a freeze," Chana says. "Thursday night it's supposed to
freeze." Chana is standing at the kitchen island, looking over her
computer at AccuWeather. "And we might get some snow at the

beginning of next week. That would be so awesome!" she says as she turns to Huang, her face all lit up.

The Li family liked to cook and go to the farmers' market together. Those were their family fun times. Chana had come home for Thanksgiving break, although her family didn't celebrate the extermination of indigenous peoples or anything that had to do with that. Rather, their celebration was about the harvest and preparing for the darkness that would set in before the light returned.

"You need more clothes." Everyone stops and looks at Grandma Luani. Luani Han seldom spoke. She has a very persistent, quiet way about her and is always watching with her large, Asian eyes.

Chana walks over and kisses her grandma.

"Okay, Grandma, but only for you." Chana runs upstairs to grab a sweatshirt jacket so her grandmother will be more comfortable. Showing so much skin is not acceptable in her grandmother's world, even if it's just arms and chest.

Chana stops to look at herself in the long mirror in her mother's room. She zips up the jacket but keeps standing in front of the mirror. She notices that she is looking heavier. She turns sideways and runs her hands over her belly, smoothing the sweatshirt jacket downward to get a better look at her profile. *I must be late with my period.*

She stands there and thinks back to her last menstrual cycle. She had been having it during her psych exam, because she can remember the cramps. She walks over to the calendar hanging next to her mother's desk. *Six weeks ago.*

Chana feels confused. Maybe she had overdone it with her running this last month. She loved her evening jogs up into the hills and sometimes into Forest Park. She makes a mental note not to jog so much for a week and see if she gets her period.

Running back down the stairs, she almost knocks her mother over on the landing.

June makes direct eye contact with her daughter. "You look very beautiful," she says to Chana.

"Ah, thanks, Mom. I was just worrying I was gaining weight, but then realized I haven't had my period yet, so it's probably just water gain."

June nods and starts heading up the stairs. "When did you have your last period?" she asks nonchalantly.

"It's been six weeks, but I think it's because I was over-jogging last month. It will probably start if I just slow down some. School has been stressful, too. I've been feeling anxious in the mornings, like I'm going to be sick. I think I've just been pressuring myself to do well on exams." Chana turns back to her mother and smiles. "Why?"

June comes back down the stairs and looks at Chana. "You'd tell me if you were in trouble, right?"

"I'm not in trouble, Mom. That's enough. I don't want to have this conversation." Chana walks off, somewhat miffed. How could her mother think she would be having sexual intercourse when she didn't even have a boyfriend? Her mother knew that school meant everything to her and that doing well was important to her "life plan."

Chana was frequently talking with June and Huang about her life plan. She wanted to become an environmental engineer and create spaces for people to grow food that could withstand the coming climate disaster, of which she had seen evidence all around. She and her parents would talk about the constant Western wildfires that would begin in late spring and extend into late fall, sending smoke everywhere, including the city of Portland, sometimes making going outside almost intolerable.

When Chana was a child, the fires would come only once in a while, but now it was every summer and fall. Last year the smoke had continued on into winter. "And no one should be having children," Chana had said during one of these long discussions. "Seven billion people on Earth, and we're worried about whether a woman has an abortion or not!? That's insanity!"

Chana's parents would be saddened to learn of their daughter's belief that humans should stop reproducing to save the planet. It was a huge part of her life plan. And she had eschewed having a boyfriend or any romantic interests, and focused only on her studies.

During one of their long discussions, Chana had said to her parents, "Someday, men will become nonexistent—assuming we manage to survive climate change and turn our Earth's temperature around. I learned in biology class that men's 'Y' chromosome is considered recessive, and if we are still here in thirty thousand years, it will have dropped out by then, making us all one sex."

Her parents had listened respectfully but told Chana they doubted that men would disappear from Earth.

"Why do you doubt it?" Chana had argued. "All of Earth's problems start with men's need to own, subdue, dominate, and rule. Without them, we might have a shot at some peace."

"But how would the human race go on if we couldn't reproduce? We need men to reproduce," June had reminded her daughter blithely.

Until now, Grandma Luani had merely sat and smiled during the discussion. "Too bad," she had said, and everyone had stopped and looked at her. Then they had all laughed loudly while Luani smiled and moved her head from side to side, the way she did.

"Come on, we're going to be late for the market," Huang yells. "I'll meet you guys out in the car. I'm walking out with Grandma, and we'll wait out there." He opens the front door and offers his arm to his mother-in-law.

They walk to the car, admiring the beautiful, sunny day. Chana makes her way into the kitchen and picks up the large market bags for their produce.

"I'm heading out to the car, Mom, are you coming?"

June comes slowly down the stairs. "I'm coming, I'm coming."

T
HE PORTLAND FARMERS' MARKET is in full swing when Sharina and Paul step off the street car, a few blocks away
from the entrance.

"We're in need of some time to just relax, Paul," Sharina had
said when Paul came in and told her about the man outside their
apartment. "Let's do something to get out into this day and enjoy
it. The smoke has finally cleared and it's going to be a nice day."
Noting that their refrigerator was looking a little empty, they had
decided to make a trip to the market.

The fall vegetables and fruits are many in the West this time of
year. There are all kinds of squashes, and there are tomatoes and
even strawberries still coming on, with the days being so unusually
warm.

Sharina heads toward a booth selling several varieties of local,
wild-crafted mushrooms. The older woman behind the table looks
up at Sharina as she approaches. The vendor is wearing a bright
red scarf around her neck that hangs down low, with small bells
on some of the fringe. She smiles at Sharina.

"How do you get your mushrooms so large and beautiful?" Sharina says as she admires the table full of goods.

"Hard work and magic," the woman replies. "*You* have magic," she says, nodding toward Sharina, who continues to peruse the table in front of her.

"Pardon me?" Sharina stops and looks up at the woman. The crowd and the buskers are loud, and she wonders whether she has heard the woman correctly. Their eyes meet.

"You have magic," the woman says again, nodding toward Sharina's middle.

This truly surprises Sharina because she is barely showing at all. She places a hand on her stomach and looks up at the old woman. "How did you know?"

"Oh, we know more than we let ourselves understand. We've lost our magic because we believe too much in technology and we have stepped too far outside of Nature."

"Yes, I agree with that," Sharina smiles.

"Just because we can explain something with science doesn't mean it isn't magical. Science has a lot of trouble keeping pace with Nature's magic. Trust me," the woman says, laying her hand on Sharina's arm.

Paul walks over to the table as Sharina is placing the quart of 'shrooms into her shopping bag. "Hey, a vendor down the road has wonderful strawberries," Paul says.

Sharina is watching the old woman. "What?" she says to Paul. "I'm sorry, what did you say?"

"I said there's a vendor with fresh organic strawberries just a ways down the road." Paul points in the direction of the booth.

Sharina hands the woman a twenty and, as the woman hands back a couple ones, she touches Sharina's hand.

"I see it. You have magic." She holds Sharina's hand a moment, then moves on to her next buyer.

Sharina steps back from the table, smiling.

"What was *that* about?" Paul asks.

Sharina hands the shopping bag to Paul, smiles at him, and the two head in the direction Paul has come from. As they make their way down the middle of the market, the crowd automatically moves in directional paths to help the flow. Sharina tries to stay on the right side of the road between the booths, to avoid running into people traveling the opposite way. The wind picks up and Sharina feels her whole body begin to tingle.

"Can I have a sip of that water?" she asks Paul, who is carrying a water bottle for them.

He looks at her. "Are you okay?"

"I feel weird," she says. "It's as if I have electricity running through me."

"Here," Paul says, handing her the bottle. "Let's go sit down for a while?"

Just as Paul is suggesting they find a bench to sit on, the crowd seems to slow down and become quiet, like background noise.

"What? I can't hear you," Sharina shouts out to Paul. Paul sounds like he is in a tunnel and far away. Sharina looks down the road and notices that everyone is moving very slowly. They seem blurry to her, out of focus.

"Paul, what's going on?" Sharina asks, but Paul's reply is muffled. Paul continues standing near her, apparently unable to move away.

A figure comes into focus down the road, not twenty feet from Sharina, and she notices it is clearer and brighter, standing out from all the other people. It is a young woman, like herself.

The two move toward each other as everyone around them appears to be frozen in time and far away.

"Who are you?" Sharina asks as the woman comes within several feet of her.

"I'm Chana. Who are you?"

"I'm Sharina. Do you know me?"

"No, but I feel like I do. I feel like you're part of me, and it feels very strange."

"Yes, I have that, too."

The two women raise their hands, palms facing each other, and place their palms closer. The wind whips leaves up around them in funnels that travel skyward.

"Wow! That is amazing. Do you feel that?" Chana says.

Sharina nods at her. "I do."

They move their hands closer, and just as they touch, the crowd around them stops moving. Everything is silent. Not a bird, not a car, not a plane…no sound.

"What's happening?" Chana says fearfully.

Sharina shakes her head. "I don't know, but I suspect it has something to do with us." She looks over her shoulder at Paul, who is standing about ten feet behind her, immobile. She sees that he can see her, though.

"I'm scared," Chana says.

Sharina moves closer to her and hugs her. "Don't be afraid." She brings Chana's body close to hers. Light comes out from between them and it is all they can see now. They are enveloped in a golden light. "I think bad people are following us; what do you think?" Sharina says.

Chana steps back from the light and looks at Sharina's face. "Yes, I feel that, too. We need to get out of here and go. But where?" Chana looks back at her family, standing a few feet away from her. As she moves away from Sharina, the sound begins to strengthen and return.

"Take my hand," Sharina tells Chana. She reaches down to clasp Chana's hand.

"Do you have a car here?" Sharina asks.

"Yes, but it's my parents'." Chana points to her mother and father and grandmother.

Just beyond Chana's parents, Sharina sees Mora and Aaron frozen in the farmers' market roadway. "Go touch your parents," Sharina says, "and tell them we need to get out of here in their car. We have to get out of here *now*."

While holding Sharina's hand, Chana walks over to her parents and touches her mother first. Her mother is released from her somewhat frozen state.

"Mom, we have to get out of here," Chana says, still holding Sharina's hand.

June doesn't question, but seems to be aware of the danger and the need to get away. "I have the car keys," she says. "Are *they* going to be okay?" she asks Chana as she looks at her husband and mother, frozen as if encased in some kind of time capsule.

"I think they will be fine, as soon as we get out of here," Sharina ventures. "Let's go!"

The three women hold hands and begin to walk back the way Chana's family had come in to the market. As Sharina walks past Aaron and Mora, they begin to move.

"Come on," Aaron says. "You have to get out of here!" He grabs Mora's hand, and the five of them make their way to the black Jeep. June jumps in behind the wheel, and the others jump into the seats and fasten their belts.

"Go, Mom!" Chana says. "Drive to Forest Park. We'll be safe there, I know it somehow." Chana looks at Sharina, who nods in the affirmative.

"Yes, that's a good place to go."

"What is happening?" Mora says as the car moves through the other cars, all frozen in a state of pause. As they begin to drive away, they see everything beginning to move again at its normal tempo.

"No one is following us," Aaron says, looking out the back window.

The five sit silent in the car as June drives to Forest Park, Sharina still holding Chana's hand behind the front seat.

***

Forest Park is 5,200 acres of managed wilderness plunked in the middle of a metropolitan area. It is a wildlife refuge and provides habitat for an immense variety of plant species. It also contains more than eighty miles of hiking trails, so one could easily get lost inside the park.

June's Jeep enters the park from Thurman Street on the northwest corner. They park in the first lot, which is a ways back into the park. It is silent in the car as everyone just sits and calms down.

"Would you please roll down my window?" Sharina asks June from the backseat. The window slides down halfway. "Everyone needs to stay calm," Sharina says, "and I'm sure we can figure this thing out." Rain clouds start to form overhead, obscuring what is left of their beautiful November day.

"We were frozen," Mora says. "I couldn't move, but I could see you," she says, turning her head toward Aaron.

"Yes, I felt that way, too. But I didn't feel scared, and I was suddenly aware that you guys were all around me." Aaron looks at the others in the car. "I'm sorry. I'm Aaron Lambert, and this is my wife Mora."

"June Li, and my daughter Chana." June looks at Sharina for an introduction, but it is Chana who speaks.

"Your name is Sharina. Why do I know your name? I've never met you before, have I?"

"No, I don't think so. But I feel the same, as if I've known you forever." Sharina smiles at Chana. "But I'm sure we've never met."

The Jeep's windows are starting to fog up inside, so June opens her door and steps out. Everyone follows. Standing next to the Jeep, Sharina tries to use her cell phone.

"It won't work up here," Chana says. "My family spends weekends here, and cell service is very spotty but you can get it to work closer to the road."

"What happened back there?" Mora asks.

Chana walks over to where Sharina is standing. "You're pregnant," she says, and lightly touches Sharina on her stomach area.

"Yes," Sharina nods. "And so are you." Sharina lightly touches Chana on her stomach but Chana pulls away.

"It's impossible! I've never been with a man before." Chana turns and looks back at her mother. "Never, Mom. I swear!"

"You didn't have to be with a man," Sharina says. "You're parthenogenic, like me. We're the same that way, and for some reason we're supposed to be together." Sharina explains her phone conversations with the lab and with Dr. Porter, who was helping Sharina understand what had taken place in her uterus.

"The Dr. Porter my dad works with?" Chana asks.

Before Sharina can answer, Mora cuts her off. "No offense, Sharina, but that sounds crazy and unbelievable. I've never heard of anyone with that ability before, and here we have two young women with the same miracle? And you guys aren't even related, are you?" Mora's eyes go back and forth between the two young women, as they shake their heads in the negative.

"I don't even want children," Chana says, her voice cracking as if ready to break down.

"Look, we need to stay calm, like Sharina said," Aaron interrupts. "Let's drive the car back out a ways and see if we can get better reception near the road."

Everyone seems to be in agreement as they load back into the Jeep.

It isn't far before the cell service bars on their phones all go from zero to one, then two. June pulls over. Everyone gets out and sits near the car.

Chana's phone rings. It's Huang and Grandma Luani, calling to find out where June and Chana had gone off to. Chana tries to explain to her dad without alarming him. "We're fine, Dad. We had something happen, and Mom and I needed to take a walk. I should have called and let you and Grandma know. We went to Forest Park. We were done with the market. I knew you guys would take the streetcar once you saw that the Jeep was gone."

Huang is upset. It wasn't like June to take Chana and not tell him where they were going.

"Let me talk to your mother," Huang says.

Chana hands the phone to June, who moves away from the car and speaks to her husband in hushed tones near a group of trees. When she returns, she stands listening to the conclusion of Sharina's conversation with Paul.

"It's like you were there and then just disappeared," Paul tells Sharina. "Where are you?"

"I'm headed home. I'll be home pretty soon. We can talk then. Not now, on the phone. Okay?"

Paul understands Sharina's need to stay off the line. "I'm going there now. I'll wait for you," he says.

When the group reassembles in the car, June is the first to speak. "I think I've found a connection between us," she says quietly, nodding toward Sharina. "You said you spoke with a 'Doctor Porter,' and my husband's boss's name is Dr. Carol Porter. Is that the same doctor you've been talking with?"

"Yes," Sharina says, "it is."

"Huang said the lab knows about your...condition, and Dr. Porter has been talking with you?"

"Yes. I have been talking with her and relaying everything to Paul. He's never met her in person. She's been a big help. We trust her."

"Well that is one connection we have. And evidently, from conversations I've had with my husband, Huang, I may have the same ability that you both have. Chana is the outcome of my…ability."

Chana turns and looks at her mother, eyes wide.

"This is crazy," Mora interrupts, flopping her arms down loudly at her sides, exasperated. "Three people in one place, all of them asexual. That's what you're saying. You're saying all three of you can reproduce without a mate?!"

The women and Aaron stand quietly. No one talks. No one moves.

Mora finally breaks the silence. "And why are we here, Aaron? What do we have to do with this?" she asks, turning to her husband.

A light suddenly comes on for Sharina. "Aaron, that day. The day you came to the rec center?" She looks at Aaron and he nods. "What made you come that particular day?"

Aaron thinks back to that strange day. He had seen it as being in response to his PTSD meltdown in the backyard. But then he remembers something that has been bothering him. "It was as if I was drawn there. I remember being in the broom closet, trying to understand what was happening and why I was there, when you opened the door. It was then that I realized you were the one who spoke to me in the spa several days before I had shipped out. I was so angry. But you know the rest." Aaron blushes and nods toward Sharina. "But it's always bothered me that I didn't know how I got there, on both days. It's just a blank and then I'm in the broom closet, and then I was in your teaching room the next week." Aaron puts his head into his hands.

"I think you were supposed to protect me, but when you saw who I was, the woman from the 2001 accidental meeting in the spa, you became distracted. You're part of this, guys," Sharina says to Mora and Aaron. "Probably more a part of this than we know."

Everyone sits in silence again.

Finally, Sharina speaks. "I need to go home. I think we should all go home and then agree to meet someplace and talk. I need to see Paul."

"Yes," June says quickly, turning to Chana. "I need to see how G'ma Luani and Dad are doing and make sure they can catch the streetcar home."

"But we all need to be vigilant and aware of what's going on around us," Aaron warns. "I'm not sure what we're watching for, but we need to be on the lookout and be very careful."

Silently the group ponders just what, exactly, they are looking out for.

"Come on," Sharina coaxes, "let's get back in the car. The doors open and they file into the seats. June starts up the engine and they roll out of Forest Park.

Just as they come to the entrance, Aaron yells out, "Everyone down," and everyone drops down onto the seats. Aaron reaches up over the back seat and puts his hat on June's head.

"Keep it on," he says.

June keeps driving.

"What is it?" Sharina asks Aaron.

"Just stay down. I don't know."

As June pulls to a stop at the entrance, a large, black van pulls in and the man who is driving looks at her. She smiles as she looks both ways before pulling out onto the main road.

Aaron's head pops up after they pass the van. "Government plates," he says. "They knew we were here."

Sharina looks at Aaron. "And you knew *they* were here."

E VERYONE SITS AROUND PAUL AND SHARINA'S apartment, trying to make sense of what had happened.

Then Paul begins pacing across the living room. "You're
a threat, Sharina. You have to look at it from a capitalistic point
of view. Once women become parthenogenic, those who pull all
the financial strings won't be able to control reproduction. Con-
trolling reproduction has historically been the right of the church,
and before that, the monarchy." Paul realizes he sounds like he's
ranting, despite his best efforts to stay calm. "The Power con-
trolled birth, not women! And having it all in women's hands is
a game changer. It's a threat!" Paul sits back down. "We have to
leave. They will come looking for you."

"Why would they come looking for *me*?" Sharina retorts. "Even
you didn't know what happened at the market, Paul. It was just a
few seconds taken from your memory, and then I was gone. If you
had been anyone else, you would've just gone on with your day
and not noticed." Sharina is lying back against the arm of the
couch, trying to stay calm.

"He's right," Aaron says from the armchair across the room.

Mora, who has been in the kitchen making tea, carries a tray with tea cups into the living room.

"Here, let me help you." Paul takes the tray and sets it down on the table. Everyone is sitting around Paul and Sharina's apartment, trying to make sense of an unbelievable situation. Paul sits down and looks around the room at everyone. He feels he's dreaming, trapped inside a late November day, and he can't cut through to the surface.

The others continue talking. June and Chana sit quietly on the couch, holding hands.

"I don't see how it's any more dangerous right now for us than it is for you with your work," Sharina says to Paul, bringing him back into the room. "You thought someone was following you about your work, and that colleague of yours had you pretty spooked a few days ago. You didn't leave and run away. Why should I?" Sharina leans forward, reaching for a cup. She pours herself some tea, then raises her cup to Mora. *Thank you*, she mouths to Mora.

The room is silent. The late afternoon sun slants inward on the group as they sit around, trying to understand.

"We've witnessed something profound," Mora says. "Why should we think we can understand it? Perhaps women have been having babies this way more than we know? Most of us give birth and never question whether the baby is our husband's making. Think of the biblical story of Mary, suddenly found with child, young and unwed. God tells the man she is to wed that it is a child of God and not to be afraid. Maybe it is a story of partho…I'm sorry, can you spell that for me?" Mora tilts her head sideways and looks at Sharina.

"P-A-R-T-H-E-N-O-G-E-N-I-C," Paul spells. "Humans aren't supposed to have this ability. I'm sure it hasn't been around for hundreds of years or we'd know. "

"But even Aaron is experiencing strange knowings," Mora points out, "and he seems to be connected to all of this in some way. It appears to be bigger than just Chana and Sharina."

June squeezes her daughter's hand. Chana reflexively reaches for Sharina's hand next to her and holds it. Before Sharina can reassure Chana that it will be okay, a light begins to form around the women's hands where they touch.

"Look!" says Sharina, nodding toward their hands.

All three look toward their hands and then toward the others. No one is moving. Everyone is frozen still in the room.

Sharina continues: "It's like at the farmers' market. When we touch, we stop time around us, or we walk into some other dimension where we are the ones missing time. Let's let go and see what happens."

The three women let go of each other's hands. No one appears to have noticed the slowdown.

Mora looks at the three of them on the couch. "What? Why are you guys looking at us?"

Sharina's phone rings, and she picks it up. "Hi, Mom," is all everyone hears Sharina say, and then her mouth closes while she listens to her mom talk. "I'll call you later," Sharina says, and hangs up.

S HARINA AND PAUL'S APARTMENT feels huge after everyone has
left. Partly to fill the space, partly to settle a pressing matter,
Sharina speaks: "Teylen says she knows what's going on and
I need to come home." She pauses and looks up at Paul. "I'm
going, Paul, and I'm hoping Chana and June will come with me."

Paul had already backed down from his argument that Vermont was too far for Sharina to drive, knowing that flying would
make her more visible.

"You stay," Sharina continues. "It's okay. I know you need to
work." She rests her hand on Paul's arm, trying to reassure him
that she won't be angry if he doesn't come with her.

"No." Paul runs his hand through his hair. "I'm coming. I can
work from anywhere, and I guess I can work from Vermont. Your
mother does have Internet, right?"

"I think so. She doesn't have a computer, but we could buy a
service if we need to. The local store also has satellite reception,
and most people go there to use their computers." Sharina winces
as she breaks the bad news to Paul. "It's very rustic where I grew

up. It's not like here." She motions across the skyline outside their large window.

"I need to think," Paul replies. "I'm going for a walk." He walks over to Sharina and kisses her lightly on the cheek. "I'll be back in an hour."

Opening the front door, Paul walks out into the hallway and looks up. "Dear God!" he says into an empty apartment hallway. He walks toward the entrance of the building, through the lobby area, and to the front door.

Stepping out onto the street, Paul notices a white stripe of masking tape across the large, blue USPS mailbox in front of his apartment. It's Collin's signal to meet up. *When it rains, it pours,* Paul thinks, reaching for his phone—but then changes his mind.

He makes the short walk to the streetcar stop and, after it slides into the benched waiting area, hops on. McMenamins is just a short ride from there. Paul watches all the people in the car sitting blankly, looking at their phones or out the windows. An older man in the back seems to be looking at Paul. Paul smiles at him.

Stepping out at his stop, Paul begins to walk toward the meeting spot and looks back. No older man following him. "I'm losing it," Paul says, walking into the restaurant. As he walks past booth after booth, expecting to find Collin, he gradually realizes Collin isn't there.

Paul spots the bartender, who has just stepped out from the kitchen area. "Excuse me," Paul says, leaning over the supersized bar. "I'm looking for a blond man about six—" but before Paul can finish his sentence, the bartender reaches under the bar for an envelope and hands it to him.

"He was here about an hour ago. Asked me to give this to you if you showed up."

"Thanks." Paul takes the envelope and sits down at the back booth. As he opens it, a waitress comes up to take his order. "Just a beer, please. Your double IPA is fine. Small pour?"

"You got it," she says. Paul pulls the letter out of its envelope and begins reading.

Paul. Couldn't wait any longer. We need a better system to connect. Next time I'll leave you a message from an anonymous IP address so we don't miss each other. I'm going to have to leave town and go under for a while. I need to talk with you. Leave a message with the bartender?

Paul looks up at the windowed area and sees the waitress bringing his beer over to him. "Thank you," he says, and hands her a ten-dollar bill. "Keep the rest," he tells her.

As the waitress strolls away, Paul takes his pen out from his coat pocket and scribbles on the back of Collin's note: *Driving to Vermont. Do you want to come? Leaving day after tomorrow, early AM. Long story. Got a place to stay and you're welcome to join us.*

He puts the letter back in the envelope and downs his beer in one gulp. "Ah, Oregon microbrew. Nothing like it," he says, wiping his mouth.

Walking over to the bar again, Paul asks the bartender for a piece of tape. The bartender hands him a tape dispenser from under the counter. Paul tapes up the back of the envelope and hands it to him. "In case he comes back?"

The bartender nods and says, "No problem," then places the envelope next to the computer screen.

"Collin. His name will be Collin." Paul hands the bartender a twenty and walks out.

D R. PORTER IS SPEECHLESS—a state in which Huang had never seen her—after Huang tells her about his wife and daughter's disappearance at the farmers' market, and about the suspension of time the two women had created, his daughter and "the woman we approached at the rec center."

"Sharina Mathews," Dr. Porter says, filling in the missing name for Huang. "I think you should bring your daughter and her mother in for testing, Huang. This is unbelievable to have found three women with this ability, all here. Something bigger is happening, and we are in the middle of it." A look of elation brightens her face.

"No," Huang replies sharply. "We are leaving. You are the only person I will tell where we'll be, but we are leaving and we will be hiding. Too much interest will be generated, and we need to be as secretive as possible if we're going to make an escape. We're going to Sharina's mom's place in Vermont."

Dr. Porter's disappointment registers strongly across her brow. Then she looks up at Huang. "So you're giving me notice that you're leaving, but you can work from Vermont? We'll stay connected?" Her voice is hopeful.

"Too dangerous," Huang says. "You must tell anyone who comes looking for me that I left and you don't know where I went. I know I can trust you, Carol." Huang had rarely called Porter by her first name. He knew she had come to count on his expertise in the lab. "I will set up a secret, untraceable account once we settle, and I will keep you up to date."

Dr. Porter hates to see her favorite, long-time researcher leave. "I understand," she says. "It's your family. I'll miss you."

Huang smiles. "And me, you. Thank you for all you've taught me here and the opportunities."

The two stand.

"Wait," Dr. Porter says. "You'll need a vehicle that isn't yours. Leave your Jeep out back and take my camper truck. It belonged to my ex and is still in his name. They'll never make the connection if they come looking for you. I think the two vehicles are pretty much of equal value. What do you think?" Dr. Porter looks over the top of her glasses at Huang.

"You're right," Huang says. "I didn't even think of that. How will I repay you?"

"Oh, I'm not doing this out of the goodness of my heart, if that's what you're thinking. I want to be kept abreast of every single thing that goes on with these women, Huang Li. You understand?"

Huang nods somberly.

"I'm keeping you on payroll, too," Dr. Porter adds, "and saying you're on vacation with your family, should anyone come looking. So now you *really* owe me."

The two laugh a little and then look at each other.

"Go!" Dr. Porter says to her assistant as she removes keys from her fob. "Go now," she says as she tosses it to him. Catching the fob, Huang lays his down on the table gently and begins to leave. Turning back, he hugs his boss. "Thank you again. I will be checking in as soon as we land. I'm glad you're in this, too. I need all the good minds I can get."

Huang opens the door quickly and steps out. As he walks toward the parking lot, he flashes back on a memory from his high-school years. Something about the hallway leading to the parking lot. Being intersexed had been easier for him than it had been for many he knew, whose gender issues had led to abuse at the hands of their peers. The male assignment had come at birth, and his gender assignment wasn't something he had gotten to decide. That's just the way it was back then. He knew that didn't always work out well, but for him it had been a life saver. He had watched others who were on the gender spectrum suffer horribly at the hands of ignorant, narrow-minded high schoolers. For him, the choices his parents had made early on had saved his life. "It could have gone the other way," he thinks out loud. "What if they had been wrong?"

Stepping out into the light, he sees Dr. Porter's ex's truck. It is huge. He climbs in and surveys the amount of room inside. The camper would come in handy for his burgeoning family. It is fully equipped, and Huang knows instantly that he has gotten the better part of the car swap.

Getting in behind the wheel, Huang texts June and tells her to be ready to leave by the day after tomorrow.

Already packing, she responds.

T EYLEN, MINKI, AND LISA HURRY around their houses, getting ready for the guests. Teylen doesn't have to explain to
her friends why they are coming. Her friends had felt the
immediacy in her voice yesterday when she asked if they could
make room. They were excited to be a part of something, and
both Minki and Lisa had good-sized farm houses, empty since
their families had moved into cities. Their gardens had been prepared for winter, but there were still some stubborn squash popping through the leaf mulch, and in the greenhouse, cucumbers
and greens persisted. Lisa's mushroom operation was in full swing
this time of year, providing epicurean delights to several upscale
restaurants around the state.

"It's another world at my ma's place," Sharina had tried to
warn Paul, who had never left the Pacific Northwest. He was used
to cities, and the concept of "rural" hadn't yet registered in his
brain.

Sharina was still shaken by what had happened at the farmers'
market and then later at her apartment. She, Chana, and June
had agreed to stay apart until they understood it better.

"What if slowing things down hurts the baby?" Chana had asked, when they were all holding hands on the couch, trying out their newfound ability. They had immediately let go and looked at each other.

"Chana's right," Sharina had replied. "Until we know what it is, we need to be careful."

And so the women had just busied themselves preparing for the cross-country trip. Flying would mean leaving a trail that could be followed, but paying cash for gas and driving would be hard to trace. Everyone bought a burner cell and turned off their smartphones. Sharina and Collin stood by the truck's door with a lockbox open for Huang, June, Chana, Mora, and Aaron to place their cell phones into, along with Collin's, Sharina's and Paul's.

"Just one person using their smartphone could ruin everything," Collin says. "It's too big of a risk."

And everyone agrees. Collin is in Paul and Sharina's newly purchased, used, thirty-foot motor home, ready to go. He had decided his job could be done from anywhere, and that a move would ensure safety for his brother and sister-in-law. He had jumped at the chance when he read Paul's letter, left at the bar. He had never lived anywhere but the West Coast, and he was excited by the idea of seeing something new. Collin hadn't been aware of the peculiarity of Sharina's and Chana's pregnancies. He was under the impression that Paul and Sharina were taking a trip with some friends, Aaron and Mora Lambert.

Three five-gallon jugs of water are in back of the RV, and both vehicles are equipped with plug-in fridge/freezers, which Sharina has loaded with sandwiches and frozen casserole dishes she had been making for the past twenty-four hours. They had done their best to think of everything they would need, so stops along the way could be brief, just long enough to gas up.

Mora had given notice at the hospital that she would be using her accumulated vacation time for a family emergency. Quitting her job was too big of a decision to make at this point. But she was amazed at the difference in Aaron since the farmers' market day. He was his old self and full of energy. She had promised herself that she would move in whatever direction helped heal her husband, and this was it.

And so all of them, for what they thought were different reasons, gradually made their way over the Great Divide and out to the Northeast, where Teylen's farm sat quietly among the green, rolling hills just outside of Barton, Vermont.

"You're from what Native tribe?" Aaron had asked Sharina during one of the long conversations they had kept going, on the trip over.

"My people are from many tribes that make up an area in what is called the Northeast Kingdom," Sharina had replied. "Those very different tribes come under one name because of the geographic area they lived in. We are collectively referred to as Abenaki. The government tried to convince the local Europeans that we were no longer. But my tribespeople organized and made it known that the Abenaki still exist, and we still have customs and a language."

As the group continues along the truck route across the country, Sharina gradually brings Mora and Aaron up to date on who her mother's people were and what the farm life would be like.

While driving through the Midwest, Chana says to her parents and Grandma Luani, "The heartland seems to be missing its heart. Everyone looks so grumpy and unhealthy."

"I don't think you can make an accurate assessment of the Midwest based only on our stopping at some gas stations along the truck route," her father counters. *But she is correct*, he thinks. *Lurking about every gas station is a slew of unhealthy-looking people who seem lost in their lives and thoughts. No one looks anyone else in the eye, and few, if any, smile when I come in to gas up.* "It is a solemn bunch, though, I will give you that!" Huang says as he turns his head back toward the passengers in the rear seats.

Huang had let Chana take a turn at the driving. June also drove for part of the long journey. Grandma Luani surprised everyone with how talkative she had become on the trip.

"When I was a girl, my family left Taiwan to escape the war," she had told them. "The town I lived in had been bombed, and we left behind everything to flee from the city. We were only allowed to take what we could carry on our backs, and we were loaded onto huge boats that brought us to America. My parents were terrified but hopeful for new lives in America. The trip was long and I was often frightened…" She was keeping everyone spellbound with the tales of her trans-Pacific trip, fleeing war and persecution.

"I didn't know any of that about you, Grandma," Chana says, looking back over the front seat at her grandmother, who is sitting next to her mother. "How come you never told me the whole story before?"

"You always busy," Luani says in deliberate Taiwan-American speak. "No time for long story."

Everyone is laughing.

It feels good to laugh, Chana thinks to herself. She runs her hand over her belly and catches her mother looking at her. They smile at each other. They had performed an at-home pregnancy test and it had shown positive. Then there had been a lot of truth unloading as her father told everyone about his birth surgery that decided his gender, and June had struggled to grasp that Chana was a product of her DNA alone. Dr. Porter's work had been helpful, and Huang's research made him a font of information that encouraged them all to understand what was going on, but no one could deny it was a miracle that would never be fully explained.

"Science can only go so fast," Huang had said, "and maybe humans are evolving at a rate that science can't keep up with. Like we're running out of time, so Nature stepped on the gas."

There had been many such conversations in their vehicle on the trip over the mountains and through the flatlands. But at the end of each one, the group had fallen back into silence. There truly was nothing that could have prepared any of them for what they were experiencing, and they were just going to have to keep going with what they knew.

Chana reaches over the seat to take her mother's hand, and June reaches for Luani's hand.

"This is a fun adventure," Grandmother says. "No need to worry. This baby is a good thing." She smiles at her granddaughter. When the three touch, there is an energy passing between them that they all feel but cannot explain. But without Sharina in the mix, there is nothing supernatural.

"The supernatural is what inhabits the space between all that we know and all that we want to know, but don't know yet." Sharina said during one of her talks with the women, trying to comfort herself as much as the others.

At night during the long journey, the group would pull in to a rest stop and the women—Sharina, June, Chana, G'ma Luani, and Mora—would get out of their vehicles and head to the restrooms. They would take turns standing watch outside, not allowing anyone in, while the women took sponge baths in the sinks, arranging their hair, and applying lotion.

During one such stop, everyone wanted to hear more about Sharina's farm. "We don't have a lot of animals, just chickens," Sharina says. "My mother used to have someone from town help with the farm, and we had animals then. Now she only has the chickens."

Sharina is worried about Teylen's ways, talking to her animals and believing they brought her "messages." She is sure the others would be unable to navigate the strange world that is her mother's. But the women are becoming friends on the trip, and Sharina finds herself embracing each one as an integral part of this geographical-spiritual journey.

EYLEN KEEPS WATCH FROM HER front window, waiting for the two vehicles to crest the hill that leads onto her property. It isn't until just before sunset, around four p.m., that she finally makes out headlights coming up over the rim.

She grabs up her coat, gently nudges Mr. Biscuit back into the kitchen, and shuts the door. Standing in the mudroom of her little house, she says a prayer, asking that her daughter forgive her for not telling her sooner. Then she throws her coat on and opens the side door to her house, stepping out on the stones that lead to the driveway.

She clicks on her flashlight and waves it as the first vehicle, the small RV, comes up over the road and toward her driveway. The driver flashes its lights at Teylen. A camper truck follows close behind.

Suddenly, everyone is getting out of the two vehicles and introductions are being made. Collin stands back a little, feeling slightly out of place on the open farm with all these virtual strangers.

"And this is Collin," Paul says, reaching back for his friend standing behind him.

"Hello," Collin says, extending his hand to shake Teylen's. "Thank you very much for having us here."

"Oh, you're most welcome," Teylen replies, "but you might change your mind when you see the work that needs to be done around this place."

Teylen nods toward Aaron and Mora, as Sharina introduces them. She then takes Luani's hand and walks with her into her house. "Let's go inside, and I will make us some hot tea." She can see weariness in G'ma Luani's eyes. "We'll let the others bring those bags in." As the two older women pass by Sharina, Teylen touches Sharina's arm. "Love you, daughter," she says in passing. "So glad you're home."

Sharina doesn't know what to make of her mother. She had phoned saying she knew something big was happening, and that if Sharina came home she would help her understand. But Sharina is in no hurry to unburden her mother of that story. It feels so good to be home and hear the familiar sounds and smell the familiar smells of her childhood home, and to share it all with Paul.

Everyone slowly makes their way into Teylen's house to gather for a meal and some much-needed showers. "We stopped every third day for showers," Chana explains to Teylen. "I don't think I could stand it much longer than that. I'm so used to showering every day before school." Chana's smile fades and she looks at the others. She is missing her school so much, missing her friends.

Mora, sitting next to Chana, reaches over to touch her arm. "You'll have so many great things to tell all your friends when you return," Mora says to Chana. "You drove across the country, and now you're living on a small farm. You'll see. You are developing an aura of mystery, suddenly being gone like that."

Chana smiles tentatively at Mora.

"This stew is amazing," Aaron says to Teylen.

"Oh, that is Minki's stew she brought over for you guys. Minki and Lisa will be coming over later and taking you guys to their place to stay. They live just down the road."

"Well, if she can make stew like this, I'm going to be very excited about staying there," Aaron says.

"He thinks with his stomach," Mora tells Teylen with a wink.

"We can work out who stays where after dinner," Teylen offers.

Sharina gets up out of her chair and walks over to Chana. "Are you finished eating? Want to go for a walk?" The two sneak out while the others are eating and drinking and relaxing. The front yard of the small farm is shrouded in darkness, having no street lights or even the distant glow of city lights.

"Wow," Chana says to Sharina, pointing up at the stars. "Look at that. I can see so many stars. And I'm pretty sure that one there is a planet! I've never been able to see the Milky Way like this and all these stars. It's so beautiful!" She turns her sweet face toward Sharina, who smiles at her.

"Yes, it is beautiful." There is silence while they walk out to the road and begin strolling toward Minki's farm. "Are you afraid?" Sharina asks as they make their way carefully in the darkness.

"I was, but I think I'm feeling better now that I've connected with you," Chana replies. "We're just so young to be having children. I still have a lot of school ahead of me."

"I know, right?" Sharina says. "Well, just because you have a baby doesn't mean you can't do school. And there seems to be a lot of people interested in helping us, so I'm sure you will return to school before you know it. You'll just return a mother and a wiser woman." Sharina smiles toward Chana in the dark.

"I'm the head of a zero-population club," Chana says. "I'm pretty sure a baby is going to lose me my position in that group. And a baby at eighteen years old! Who's going to believe me if I tell them I've never had sex but I'm pregnant?"

The two keep walking through the dark night along the road. "*I* can't even believe it," Chana adds. "And what's to say it won't keep happening? I'm not like that Mary woman in the Bible who had a son and he became famous. Everyone believed her. Christians worship her, but if she were here today, they'd just call her a liar—or worse. And I'm not religious at all, so why me?" The two young women walk along in silence for while.

"I don't know, Chana, but I do know it's kind of exciting to be where we are. We're special, somehow, and I'm glad I'm not on this path alone. I don't think I could do it without you."

The two hold hands and continue walking. A faint, golden glow can be seen in the dark as they head toward Minki's farm.

S HARINA AND CHANA SIT at the large table in Minki's kitchen. "Your mom is so lucky to have you come visit and bring so many friends," Minki says to Sharina.

Sharina starts to explain things to Minki, but Minki interrupts. "No need to explain to me. I'm just an old woman and I'm always glad for company. We used to sit around this table and tell stories. Your mom and I still do sometimes. Old Indian stories from our people. You know how she loves the storytelling tradition, Sha?"

Minki is right. Teylen is all about the old ways and the stories that her people had handed down. Turning to Chana, Sharina explains oral tradition. "Native culture teaches the importance of oral telling over the written word. Oral teachings like those of the Buddha, Socrates, or even of Christ were right-brained, more based in the female world."

"So, Jesus didn't write any of the Bible?" Chana asks.

"Not a word," Minki replies. "Jesus was a right-brained, oral storytelling man whose words were capitalized on long after his death. That is, if one believe Jesus was a real person who walked Earth." Minki pours the young women another cup of tea, then takes up her knitting. "When men created the written word, they switched on the left side of the brain, and women suffered where once they were Goddesses. Always this battle between the linear, abstract, masculine thinking and the image-based, healing, holistic feminine thought."

Sharina had heard all of this before, but Chana sits with eyes wide, taking in Minki's words.

"Even today in politics we see this battle," Minki says, looking over the top of her glasses. "From the quest to create artificial intelligence, and thus artificial life, to the abortion issue at the center of the battle between male God and female Goddess. Trying to take away women's control over their natural ability to bring forth life is fundamental to taking away women's power. Women creating offspring with no male needed..." Minki looks up at Chana, "...well, that speaks to whose side Nature is on." She glances at Sharina with a smile.

Sharina turns to Chana. "Oral storytelling is vital to any culture that wishes to preserve women as powerful."

"My favorite story," Minki adds, "is about the Spirit that comes down from the stars and holds a little Abenaki girl just a few inches off the ground. No one believes she could be special, so they can't see that she floats."

Sharina smiles and bounces her eyebrows at Chana while the two sip their tea.

Minki continues, "This angers the spirit, so when the child is older, it decides to give the young woman a child, part Native child but also part Astral child. As the child grows inside the young woman, everyone thinks she is a bad tribal member because she has become pregnant without a husband. They push her out of their tribe and they make her live among the animals in the forest. The animals love the young woman and she loves the animals. They quickly become her family—and she, theirs. The baby is born deep in the forest, and after it is born, the stars shine down where the baby lies in the mother's arms and the animals all gather and settle down around the mother and child. Each animal brings food and takes the child as their own. She is a child of Earth and a child of the stars."

"This story sounds very familiar," Chana interrupts.

"Well, yes," Minki says, quickly looking up from the knitting that is busying her hands. "Many stories like this. Must be true." Minki sets her knitting down on the table and picks up the teapot. "More tea?"

COLLIN, PAUL, AARON, AND HUANG sit around the fire pit in Teylen's yard, talking about all that is happening in their lives. The fire leaps high at first, but eventually settles down as night descends.

"I'm just glad I don't have to get in the RV tomorrow," Collin says as he takes a sip off the beer they are sharing. Teylen had only two beers on hand, so the guys are making it stretch as far as possible.

"So your work and Paul's work intersect somehow?" Huang asks Collin and Paul. "How is this, when you don't work for the same company?"

Collin begins to explain to Huang about the job he and Paul had both interviewed for, and about the subsequent job he had landed at the DOD, through Paul's boss at Axis Software.

"It all got a little too real when Paul and I began to suspect we were working on some type of weapon that we don't fully understand," Collin says. "Because we were compartmentalized by our places of employment. When we started to ask questions, we both got pushback. Some very serious pushback, on my end." Collin reaches for the beer from Paul, who hands it to him. "To Sneakers, my cat," Collin says as he holds the beer up toward the heavens, then takes a sip. The men sit quietly.

"How about you, Huang?" Aaron asks. "Your work sounds pretty interesting, studying genetic abnormalities and working in a research laboratory?"

"Well, it may sound interesting but I assure you, most of the time it's super tedious and somewhat boring. It wasn't until I acquired Sharina's file that some of the answers I've been searching for finally came to me. That part is very interesting." Huang offers the beer he is sipping on to Paul.

"I'm good," Paul says. "You guys finish it."

"What led you into that field?" Aaron continues.

Huang hesitates, then looks at each of the men. Flashing back to high-school times and the cruelties his male classmates exacted on anyone who happened to be different, he decides to risk it. "I was born intersexed," he says.

No one moves, and the night suddenly seems even quieter than it was before. The fire pops, shooting sparks up into the cold darkness, and the three men lean back, away from the fire.

"Oh," Aaron says finally. "I'm not sure I understand what that means."

"Well," Huang replies, "it means I was born with both male and female biological traits, including an extra 'X' chromosome. But my parents decided at birth that I was male, and they had the surgery performed on me. I grew up male, never questioning my maleness, until I hit puberty and needed to start taking hormones to ensure that my growth continued in the direction my parents had set out for me at birth. I was lucky, because they had guessed right. I identified as male before I even knew about the surgery. Lots of babies aren't so lucky." Huang picks up a stick and pokes at the fire. "Today when a baby is born intersexed, the parents sometimes wait until the child is old enough to know what sex he or she identifies with. Some kids grow up and never choose. They identify with their intersexed being and with both genders."

"Wow!" Aaron says out loud, and then catches himself. "I'm sorry, I didn't mean to say that. It's just amazing what you have gone through, and some of it the moment you were born. That's rough."

"I suppose," Huang says, "but I've always felt lucky. I had never told June that I couldn't biologically make a family, and when she told me she was pregnant I didn't question her. I came to believe that she hadn't been with anyone but me, and so I went looking for the answers through my research." Huang takes another sip of the beer.

The men sit in silence for a while. Finally Huang adds, "While that provided me with some answers, it has also opened up lots of new questions."

"Don't I know that one!" Collin commiserates. "Trying to find answers but just coming up with more questions. Maybe the questions are more important than the answers?"

The men continue to rehash stories of the trip across the country as they finish up the two beers. The stars are brilliant in the sky and the night is crisp. In the garden, small seeds sleep under the mulch, waiting for winter and then the return of warmth and spring. The land spreads out around the farm and the world moves through the heavens.

T EYLEN STANDS OUTSIDE HER HOUSE and looks up at the large, gray dish that has been affixed to one corner of her roof. "It looks like you're trying to talk to outer space," she comments to Paul after the rig has gone up.

"We are," Paul replies as he walks toward the tractor in Teylen's barn. "Thank you for letting us install it. It allows Collin and me to complete our work without anyone knowing where we're working from."

"Well, they would certainly be surprised to know it was from here," Teylen responds as she watches Paul head toward the tractor. "You going to fire that tractor up?"

"Yes. I thought I would move the mulch pile on the east corner and apply it to your grapes and raspberries, like you mentioned last evening."

"Great!" Teylen loves having strong men around to help with the farm chores. And Sha's man is a good one. She likes him and understands what Sha sees in him. Putting her hands in her pockets, she walks back through the mudroom door. She sees Sharina at the kitchen sink, washing the breakfast dishes. Teylen removes her shoes and stands next to her daughter at the sink.

Sharina side-eyes her mother. "We haven't really spoken since we got here two days ago," she says. "You said on the phone you could help me understand what's going on with me and Chana."

Teylen smiles at Sharina, a big smile. She picks up a towel and begins drying pans.

"Well?" Sharina says. "*Now* might be good."

"I only knew your father for a very short amount of time," Teylen begins, "and I was young, like you. I visited him on this farm that he owned, which at that time also included Minki's farm and Lisa's farm. He was working on the houses on all three farms and getting ready to sell the place. We had only slept together once when I discovered I was pregnant with you. He tried to make everything okay for me and make me feel safe here, and I did feel safe here, so I stayed. But he was not a family man. He was a wanderer and had inherited this property from his family.

"We had initially met in town, at the trailhead, and had just started talking as we hiked. I was instantly attracted to him, and him to me. After several months of him trying to be here with my belly growing and the inevitability of your pending birth, he became agitated and didn't want to be here any longer. He signed the farm parcels over to me, and he left. That was that. I woke up one morning and he was gone, and I was the owner of this small farm and the two next door."

Teylen takes the last pan from Sharina and finishes drying it off. Sharina stops doing the dishes and sits down at the table. Teylen moves to the table and sits next to her. Sharina can see the subject is a difficult one for her mother. Teylen looks around the room and then at her daughter.

"I met Minki in school, and Lisa is her cousin. They were regulars at the tribal meetings I was attending, and we became friends while growing up and then as adults. They needed a place to live, and I needed other people to take care of these places out here. So they both moved into one of the small houses. As I grew larger with the pregnancy, it was good to have women friends around and close by.

"We needed to earn enough to support the farms' taxes and updates, so we started growing fruits, and Lisa began a mushroom operation on her farm piece. Between the three farms, there was enough income to support the three of us."

Teylen lays her hands on the table. It was rare for Sharina to see those hands not moving, not doing something.

"The night you came," Teylen continues, "I had something quite unusual happen. Minki and Lisa were here, and we were all very involved in your birth. Lisa stood by my bed and did our tribal singing and kept herbs burning in the next room, herbs that help with the pain of birth. It was a long labor, but then you started to come out. Just as your head came into view, everything froze in the room. It was as if Minki and Lisa were in suspended time and couldn't see or hear me. I was young, and it was terrifying."

"I just kept working on pushing you out. Finally I rolled over to my hands and knees, and you came out easily, in one push. You were what my tribe calls 'facing the heavens,' which means face-up, and when you slipped into this world, everything started to move again. We were so excited about you being here that we just stayed on task and didn't immediately talk about what had happened. That was easy, because the two of them were not as aware of it as I had been. But they knew they had lost time, and eventually we had that conversation. There was a warm golden glow in the room when you were born, and it was silent, as if you and I were in some capsule protected from time. I knew you were special, and Minki and Lisa knew it, too. Over the next few weeks, the golden heat generated by our touch that we had at your birth subsided, and life went on. I was so happy to have you here, but it was always in the back of my mind."

Sharina smiles at her mother and places a hand on her hand. She closes her eyes, and her hand becomes very warm where she and Teylen are touching. When she opens her eyes, her hands and Teylen's are both glowing gold, and tears are streaming down Teylen's cheeks. The two feel the warmth of the energy passing between them as they sit at the table, holding hands. "Why didn't you tell someone, Ma?"

"I just didn't know who to tell or what to do," Teylen replies, "and I worried what would happen if others found out. Some of the older tribal women knew I was without a husband, and they were very helpful. But I never said a word to anyone except Minki and Lisa." Teylen looks into Sharina's eyes. "You learned at a voracious rate. You read everything I had in the house, and we had to make twice-weekly trips in to the library. I enrolled you in a community school program where you were with other kids, but you worked at your own rate. There was just no stopping you, Rina. It was as if you had someplace to be and were following some invisible schedule that you knew about but I didn't. I just tried to stay out of your way...and love you, of course. We all loved you. Minki and Lisa were there for you always, and always will be. You know that."

Teylen gets up and walks over to where Sharina is sitting. She places her hand on Sharina's baby bump, which is just starting to show. "This one is special, too," she says. "When you use your gift, I can feel it, and it will be the same for you with this one. But people like us usually only have one and it is usually female."

"What do you mean 'people like us,' Mom?" Sharina looks up at Teylen, who is standing next to her.

"You know," Teylen replies. "We have the ability to create our own offspring—without sex. It happens when we are young, and then we cannot have any more children. There are stories in our culture about such special beings. The story my mother told me was that we were visited by heavenly spirits who knew more than humans. They were all-knowing spirits who had walked in our footsteps before us, in time. We are from them. And it's not because we are Natives. There have been such stories in other cultures, as well."

Sharina stands up. "Hug me, Ma. I'm scared." Teylen pushes her chair away as she stands up and puts her arms around Sharina, and Sharina holds onto her mother as she never has before.

"You can do this," Teylen whispers into her daughter's ear. From inside the kitchen window, a warm golden light emanates out into the evening's darkness.

GRANDMA LUANI HAS HER OWN ROOM at Minki's farmhouse. She loves looking out the window in her room and seeing the chicken yard in the back area. She had been assigned to the chickens as part of her daily chores, and while she missed the neatness of their house in the city, she was loving the cool weather and the cleaner air. And the chickens had sealed the deal for her.

She dresses quickly and meets Minki and June in the kitchen, drinking ginger tea. "Good morning," Luani says brightly.

"Good morning, Mom," June says. "Come have tea with Minki and me."

Luani eyes the tea. "I'm heading out to check on the chickens, and then I'll have tea."

The boots are just a little too large for her, but Luani can use them to go as far as the backyard. She easily slips her feet into the boots, then grabs her coat off its hook by the door.

The morning is cold and crisp, and the sun is already up. Luani opens the pumphouse door and steps down inside, where the chicken feed is kept in a small, galvanized steel garbage can. Removing the lid, she scoops up the seed in a repurposed, plastic, quart-sized yogurt container, then replaces the lid. She grabs up the egg basket on the shelf and hurries to be out of the musty-smelling pumphouse.

There is a thin leather strap that opens the back gate, and she pulls on it. The yard is fenced, but the surrounding area lends the yard the illusion of continuing all the way out to the rolling hills beyond the farm. Grandma Luani had never seen anything so beautiful in her life. She loves this place.

All the chickens come running over to where Luani stands, and she spreads the seed out on the ground for them. Then she squats down and begins petting the girls on their thick, puffed-out breast feathers. "Hello, Red; hello, Raven; hello, Beatrice; hello, Quee-nie…" Every chicken has a name, and Luani already knows each chicken by sight, despite their similar appearances. She is fascinated by how smart the birds are and how quickly she has become attached. She heads over to the coop and opens the back door on the nesting boxes. Gently reaching in, she removes each egg from the nests. The eggs are still warm.

Walking back to the pumphouse, she replaces the scoop in the can and closes the lid. She immediately hears June and Minki's voices as she enters the mudroom to remove her coat. The egg basket has about fifteen eggs in it. She sets it down carefully on the back counter where Minki had shown her. Walking over to the mudroom sink, she washes her hands and listens to the conversation.

"She was always special from the very beginning," June is telling Minki. "And so smart! Thank goodness Huang was able to keep up with her, because I couldn't. When the farmers' market miracle happened, it was the first time I had any validation that Chana was different."

Minki moves over and invites Luani to sit down next to her at the table. She reaches for the teapot and pours Luani some tea. Grandma nods in appreciation.

"I just didn't know *how* special," June continues. "And after the farmers' market, I didn't know what I was supposed to do. I guess we've been following Sharina's lead on that one. I'm just so grateful you are here," she says to Minki, smiling over the top of her teacup.

"Of course we're here!" Minki stands up, moves to the kitchen window, and looks outside. Then she turns back to June at the table. "But I suspect you do know what to do, June. In fact, I suspect you were able to do what you did at the market because you are like Chana."

June's brows come together. "Yes, I think you're right. I am like Chana. Huang and I have discussed this several times."

Almost as if on cue, Chana walks into the kitchen. "Are you talking about me?" she blurts out.

"Good morning!" Grandma Luani says, giving her granddaughter the "slow down" eye.

Chana walks over to her grandma and kisses her on the cheek. Then she walks over to her mother and asks again. "What were you guys saying about me?" She looks toward Minki standing at the counter.

"I was just telling your mother that she is like you. I think she has your abilities, and she agrees. What do you think of that, Chana?"

Chana looks at her mother, but then she picks up a banana and asks Minki if she can eat it.

"Please, eat anything you can find. I'll make us some breakfast here soon," Minki replies.

Chana peels the banana and stuffs a piece into her mouth. "I think Dad is important and I'm glad he's my dad," she says with her mouth full of banana.

Minki smiles at her. "Of course," she says, then quickly moves on. "So, what does everyone want for breakfast?" The conversation shifts to eggs and pancakes or hash browns. They decide on eggs and pancakes, and everyone gets up and chips in on preparing the meal.

***

Chana and June look at each other from across the kitchen. Everyone just keeps making the food, and Minki reaches up to the top of her refrigerator and turns on her radio. Morning instrumental music comes from her favorite channel and accompanies breakfast preparations.

THE LIGHT FROM MINKI'S FARMHOUSE can be seen out Lisa's kitchen window, just to the west. Lisa passes by the room where Collin is still sleeping and quietly pulls the door shut, so as not to wake him. Lisa notices the light is already on in Minki's kitchen, and she fills her teakettle with water and sets it aflame on her propane stove. Mora is tying up her robe as she moves into the kitchen, where Lisa is starting her morning preparations.

"Good morning, Lisa," Mora says, smiling but still half asleep. The trip across the country had not worn off yet, and the time difference was interfering with her circadian rhythms.

"Did you sleep okay in that bed, Dear?" Lisa asks, not having had any recent visitors to test the bed's comfort.

"Oh, yes," Mora replies. "We both slept like the living dead. Aaron is still in there, snoring away. I like to get up early. Just habit. Is there something I can do to help?" Mora stands by the kitchen table, looking around to see what she can do.

"You're fine. I just want to get some hot water going for tea. Get a drink of water and feel free to use the bathroom. That bathroom at the back of the house next to your room is just for your use."

"Why are you helping us, Lisa?" Mora asks. "You're being so kind, and you don't even know us." She had been wanting to ask the question since they arrived.

"I don't have to know you to know you're Sharina's friends," Lisa replies. "I love Sharina, and I know she wouldn't have bad friends. So you're my friend, too. Besides," Lisa says, smiling and turning away from the stove toward Mora, "why do you trust me? Maybe I'm an axe murderer and now I have you living in my house? Or I'm going to lock you into farm servitude for the rest of your life?"

Mora laughs. "I'd be okay with that. I really enjoy working around this place. I suppose I trust you for the same reason. Sharina. She has helped both Aaron and me so much. We've become quite close."

Lisa motions for Mora to sit down at the table, and Mora complies. Lisa sets a tea cup in front of her and says, "I'll have some tea for that in just a moment."

"Wow, thank you for making me tea in the morning. This is pretty special."

"You need to stop thanking me for everything," Lisa says, placing her hand on Mora's arm. "You guys are pulling your own weight around here, and having the extra hands to help out is wonderful! I couldn't have gotten that fence fixed that Aaron worked on yesterday, and I have you guys committed for my mushroom house update. I'm enjoying having people here to talk to and bump into. So, no more thank you's." Lisa pours Mora some tea and sits down.

The house is simple, but it does have four bedrooms, three of which no one was using until the new guests arrived. Mora notices the simplicity of the furniture, everything clean and sturdy but nothing fancy or expensive-looking. The kitchen is large, with room for a table and four chairs. There is a dining room and a living space and two bathrooms.

"I love the wide-plank hardwood floor in here," Mora says to Lisa. "Do all three houses have this?"

"Yes. All the old houses in Vermont were made that way. I love it, too. Brings a lot of life and warmth into the house."

Collin wanders out into the kitchen wearing jeans and a T-shirt. He's clean-shaven and his hair is combed. "Good morning," he says to Lisa and Mora. "I'm going to start in on that work you needed doing outside while you guys make breakfast, or I can make breakfast. I'm pretty good in the kitchen."

Collin has a nice smile, Lisa thinks to herself. *Too bad I'm not twenty years younger...*

"Do you have a preference?" Collin asks Lisa.

Lisa smiles at Collin. "How about you round up those boards from the fence job Aaron finished last night and stack them over there, by the shed." She points out her kitchen window to an empty area next to the shed.

"Sure thing, my pleasure." Collin turns on the faucet and pours himself a drink of water. "How are you feeling this morning, Mora?"

"Me? I'm fine. I'm still pondering if the hospital here is large enough for me to relocate my work. The break feels good, though, and I slept like a log last night." Mora sips her tea.

"Me, too," Collin replies. Then, to Lisa: "Felt like you drugged our food, I slept so deeply."

"Well, fresh air and physical labor does that to you," Lisa replies. "Everyone was such a big help on fixing the fence yesterday. Thank you so much."

"Ahh, no thank you's, remember?" Mora says, smiling up at Lisa while sipping her tea.

Collin grabs his coat off the hook in the mudroom and heads out. He sees the light coming from Minki's farm next door, and then Teylen's just beyond that. The morning air is cold and clear, and his breath is visible as he walks toward the stack of boards.

I wonder if I could get used to a life like this? Collin thinks to himself. *No jumping into the car and driving in the morning. No noise of the city and stinky air.* He notices how good it feels to do physical labor first thing in the morning. To stretch and just breathe. *No wonder everyone is so unhealthy,* he thinks. *They're missing out on this! There's just something so grounding about being on the land, doing physical labor early in the morning. Life feels complete—and the day is just beginning!* "And I'm not worried someone is following me, for the first time in weeks," Collin catches himself saying out loud.

After a while, Aaron sticks his head out the door and hollers at Collin to come eat. Inside, Mora, Lisa, and Aaron are working on getting the food to the table.

When Collin walks in, he can smell bacon and pancakes. "I swear, Lisa, you're making it so we'll never want to leave. You'd better be careful!" He washes up and carries a couple of mugs of hot tea over to the table.

After everyone sits down, Lisa speaks. "I'd like to say a spirit prayer for Sharina and Chana's safety. May the spirits of this world, and the spirits of all time, join together to keep these young women safe as they continue on this incredible journey." Lisa looks up and smiles at everyone. "Eat up!"

PAUL AND COLLIN HAVE MADE a makeshift room in the basement of Teylen's house. It has computers and good lighting and a drafting board for both of them to work on.

Paul's trips into Silicon Valley have been ongoing, and he's preparing to leave yet again. "I'm just worried about leaving you here alone," he tells Sharina.

"I'm hardly alone, Paul, and you need to go to these meetings to keep your job. I don't want the baby and this birth to make you lose your job." Sharina walks back and forth in the basement room where Collin and Paul work. Collin is outside with Teylen, getting some instructions on fixing the chicken coop roof before the snow sets in.

"I'm still in my first trimester with the pregnancy," Sharina continues. "Anything can happen, and I want you to have something to go back to if it does."

"What do you think is going to happen?" Paul asks.

"Nothing," Sharina replies. "I think nothing is going to happen, and then you'll want a job to return to. But if something *does* happen, we don't want to start all over. And that apartment was hard won. You know how difficult it could be to land another apartment in Portland as nice as that one." Sharina walks over to Paul and hugs him. "I love you," she says, and looks up at him. "You've been great with this. I'm so lucky I have you."

Paul kisses Sharina lightly on her forehead and then on her mouth.

"I have my mother here, and Collin will be working in the house when you're gone. Nothing will happen. I want you on that plane tomorrow to the next meeting, and call me when you get there. I worry about you, too. You and Collin seem to be pretty convinced that you're working on some type of weaponry that neither of you recognize. That's not what you signed up for. And what happens if they find out that you know? Collin seems pretty upset about what happened to his cat. So I need you to call me and let me know you're okay when you get out of the meeting. And that you're on your way back here. To me." Sharina drops her head and looks at Paul from under her lashes.

"Okay, I'll go," Paul says. "And I'll call you when the meeting is over. But you pay attention to who is coming and going down the road, and don't be so trusting of people, Sha. It scares me how quickly you accept strangers."

"I'll pay attention, but I'm pretty good with people and I think I can tell when someone is bad. But you're right, I need to be careful now. And I will."

"Hey, guys." Collin opens the door at the bottom of the stairs that leads into the basement room. "What's going on?"

"Paul was just telling me that he's going to go pack for his plane trip tomorrow," Sharina says, looking at Paul. She hugs him once again, and then turns to Collin and smiles. "And you're our watch-dog. How's that for news?"

Collin looks at Paul. "We'll be okay, Paul. I'll keep an eye out, and everyone knows to be wary. You go and check in on the other end of things, yeah?"

Paul nods. "Yes. But it's not fair when you two gang up on me!" he smiles at Collin and then at Sharina. "Come on, let's go upstairs."

Paul holds Sharina's hand, and the two move up the stairs toward the hallway at the top. Once there, Paul turns to Sharina. "I've left my phone downstairs. I'll be right back. Go ahead, and I'll come find you."

Sharina drops his hand and starts down the hallway. "Don't grill Collin too hard," she says from halfway down, turning around to give Paul "the Sha look."

Paul smiles. "I won't. I'll be right there." He turns to walk back down the wooden stairs to the basement. He opens the door at the bottom. Collin is busy at his computer. He turns around to see Paul again. Paul places his hand on Collin's shoulder. "I need to know you're going to really be aware and alert while I'm gone."

"Everything's going to be fine, Dad," Collin says, jokingly, patting Paul's hand on his shoulder. "And yes, I'm watching and being aware. Try not to worry." Collin turns back to his computer screen. "I know you love her. She'll be okay." He turns again and smiles up at Paul.

"Yeah, I guess I do love her. Do you think she'll marry me one day?" Paul asks his friend sincerely.

"I'm not the person you need to pose that question to," Collin says, turning back around and moving closer into the screen. "And I'm not sure now is the right time. Everything is about timing, with things like that. Hey, Paul. Come here and take a look at this."

Paul leans over Collin's shoulder and looks at the array of coding he's laid out. "I need to find some kind of primer for this schematic," Collin says, "so I can understand what all these codes mean."

"Sorry, Buddy. I'm upstairs packing or there'll be hell to pay." Paul pats Collin on his shoulder. "But if you leave that open when you're done, I'll come down and take a look at it when I'm all packed." Paul turns and heads back up the stairs. His plane leaves at seven a.m., and the drive into town will mean he's getting up around four a.m. to make his flight.

The details of what Paul is working on keep swimming around in his head. The deeper he gets into the project, the more he thinks Collin may be right: that they are working on some kind of weaponry that uses vibration to destroy things. "And that's a job I don't want," Paul says out loud, surprising himself.

He heads to the back of the house, pulls his rolling carry-on case from the closet, and begins to pack. *I just wish there was a way I could know.* He decides that on this trip down to Axis Software, he is going to hit Christensen up for some "bigger picture" explanations.

MINKI'S HOUSE HAD BECOME quite busy with Grandma Luani, June, Huang, and Chana living in her spare rooms. The three older women are working on chicken pot pies for a group get-together. Huang pokes his head around the corner and makes his way to the sink for water. "I'm down at the end of the hall if you need some extra help," he tells the women in the kitchen as he heads toward his makeshift office. "Just holler and I'm there," he says halfway down the hall.

June runs her ideas for the pies by the others: "I'm thinking peas, carrots, potato, celery, onion, and chicken for the filling."

"I think I have most of those ingredients here in the kitchen," Minki replies. "But the potatoes are in the root cellar, and someone will have to go get them. If we make one pie per household, it should be enough for everyone. Don't you think?" She looks up at June and G'ma Luani.

Luani nods her head. Her long hair is tied up at the nape of her neck and she is wearing Minki's red apron.

"That sounds really delicious," June says. "I think we should make four pies, though, because the men are such big eaters and if we have leftovers, that would be great. Do you have enough ingredients for four pies?" she asks Minki.

Minki starts to dig through her refrigerator drawer, counting her carrots, onions, and celery.

"I'm taking the bus to town with Sharina," Chana says as she darts through the busy kitchen. "We're going shopping for maternity clothes at the used clothing store."

All three of the older women stop what they are doing and look up.

"Stop worrying, you guys," Chana reassures them. "We have to continue living, and I need some air and room to be young. We'll be careful, and Sharina knows the town. Just relax. Do you guys need anything from town while we're there?"

Still, no one moves.

Finally, Luani speaks. "I could use some hand lotion." She gets up to retrieve her purse from the back room.

June and Minki continue watching in silence. June gets up and follows G'ma Luani to the back room, leaving Minki and Chana alone in the kitchen. As Chana turns to follow her mother, Minki smiles at her. "You two deserve some fun time. It must be stressful, being away from all your friends and everything you know."

Chana turns around and faces Minki. "I'm talking to them on my new cell phone Dad bought me under a fake name," she replies. "That is, when I can get a signal out here. It's not so bad since Sharina is here, too." She continues on toward the back room, where her mom and G'ma have disappeared to, but Minki isn't finished.

"You stay close to Sharina when you go into town," Minki says, stopping Chana in her tracks.

Chana turns around. "Why?"

"Because she knows the town, just like you said." Minki can hear the other two women talking in the back room. "Maybe give them a minute to discuss things," Minki advises Chana.

Chana comes back into the kitchen and sits down, resignedly.

When the other two women return, G'ma Luani hands Chana sixty dollars. "Use some of the money to get yourself a nice sweater for winter that will cover the baby, too." Luani puts her hand on Chana's shoulder. "Be safe, child," she says, looking over the top of her glasses.

"I will," Chana says, stuffing the money into her pocket. "Thank you, Grandma."

June walks over and hugs Chana. "See you when you get back," she says, feigning nonchalance, but she can hear the worry in her own voice.

"Okay, Mom. We'll be safe. Don't worry." Chana kisses her mother and heads out the door.

The day is cold when it first hits, Chana thinks to herself as she steps onto the stepping stones. *It feels good to be walking.* She puts her hands in her coat pockets and heads out onto the plowed road.

"Hey over there!" Mora calls from behind Lisa's small evergreen hedge that divides the properties. She waves to be sure Chana sees her.

"Mora! Come with us into town! We're taking the bus!" Chana yells across the hedgerow.

Before she knows it, Aaron and Mora are at her side, ready for the trip in to town.

Sharina comes out from inside Teylen's house. She is surprised Mora and Aaron have joined them. "If we're all staying together in town," she says to them, "I need you to know that we're shopping for maternity clothes. Might not be the most exciting thing for those of you who aren't pregnant." She puts her hair behind her ear, walking with the others up to the bus stop.

"The four of us! I think it's great," Aaron says. "We can practice as if you're our teenagers, for when we have our own kids."

Aaron's smile is so genuine that Sharina and Chana can't re-
sist him. Mora sees it. She is thankful for their friendship and for
being a part of Aaron's healing, which she seems to be witnessing
in real time each day. He just keeps getting better, more at peace
and more grounded. He is sleeping through the night and wak-
ing ready to do a day. Mora smiles at Chana. "Thanks for letting
us come with you guys," she says as she looks down the road. "I
needed a break from my computer and those online classes."

"Mora's doing her first-aid certification, and applying for the
hospital's midwife classes," Aaron says, his breath visible as he
makes the announcement.

"That's new." Sharina looks sideways at Mora as she walks. "Is
that something you've been wanting to explore?"

Mora's head bounces, keeping pace with the others. "I think
it's something I've been interested in for a long time. I just didn't
realize it until I saw these classes being offered online."

Nearing the highway, the sound of trucks and cars can be
heard. The group continues to walk toward the sound and onto
the highway.

Mora steps back from the road once they reach the bus stop.
"We should use cash for the bus fare, not our cards." She looks at
Sharina.

"Oh, the buses are all fare-free," Sharina smiles. Noting the
disbelief on their faces, she adds, "I know. It's wonderful…Hey,
look." Sharina points down the road. Everyone leans forward to
see. "Bus is coming."

P AUL TAKES THE ELEVATOR UP to the fourth floor, where his meeting with Kyle Christensen and the others will take place. He pauses a second to text Sharina. He looks at his watch and realizes it is only six a.m. on the East Coast. He decides to text her anyway. *I'm here at the meeting. Afterwards, taking a flight up to Portland to check on our apartment before returning Friday. I love you.* As he is putting the phone away, he gets a text back.

I love you, too. Chana and I going to town for maternity clothes tomorrow. See you when you return home. Be safe.

Paul worries about the two going into town, but then realizes it is inevitable. He couldn't have endured what Sharina and Chana have endured as teenagers moving into adulthood. He texts back one more time. *You're amazing. Be safe.* And then he heads for the large double doors at the end of the hall.

A booming voice comes from Paul's right. "Paul Stone. There you are!" He sees Kyle Christensen walking toward him, the large AXIS logo behind him on the wooden paneled wall. "Good to see you, Paul. Was your flight okay?" The two shake hands. Paul had caught Axis's private jet on a connecting flight out of Chicago with several other people going to California.

"Yes, it was fine—thank you, Kyle. How are you doing?" Paul opens one of the large, heavy doors and allows Christensen to move into the room. Two other men—strangers to Paul—follow behind him and also walk into the room.

"I'm doing fine, I can't complain. Work is good and family is good. I'm a lucky man! How's that girlfriend of yours doing, Paul? Everything going well in your home life?" Kyle says with a huge smile full of piano teeth opening up across his face.

Paul is immediately hit with electricity coursing through his body. Kyle has never asked about Sharina before, although Paul is aware they've talked about his living with a girlfriend.

"Yes, my girlfriend is away at a conference in Europe," Paul counters quickly. "She is well, thank you." *Keep it short and relax,* Paul thinks to himself. He turns to the strangers and puts his hand out to shake the first man's hand. "Hello, Paul Stone. I don't think we've met."

"Sihad Sanakara, nice to meet you." He shakes Paul's hand. Paul turns to the other man.

"Paul Gleeson," the other one says, shaking Paul's hand.

"So, two Pauls," Kyle clarifies loudly, then says to Paul Stone, "We'll call you Paul One, and Gleeson, you'll be Paul Two, so we don't get you guys mixed up."

Everyone sits down, and Paul One opens his computer.

"I'm bringing Sihad and Paul Two in just to get a look at the work you're doing and ask any questions they may have while you're here in town." Kyle pushes his thick hair back and adjusts his shirt collar.

"Oh, so you both work at AXIS?" Paul One asks.

"No, Paul, they don't." Kyle says curtly.

"I don't understand." Paul looks at the two men. "Then who do you work for?"

"They're both DOD, Paul. We're looking at some possible broader applications for your work. DOD has been funding several of our projects here, and when we have something they might be interested in, we share. Always good to share, right?" Kyle places a large hand on Paul's shoulder and flashes his piano teeth again.

"I'm just a little confused," Paul replies. "I thought the work I was doing was for new technology for cars and mass-transit systems. Why would the DOD be interested in it?"

"We see military applications for it," Paul Two replies. Then his lips press shut so hard, he looks like a kid who is refusing to eat his vegetables. The room sits silent for a moment.

Paul's mind is racing, but he takes a big breath and continues. "Okay," he replies, turning to Kyle. "But I can only present to you with the applications that I was designing for."

"Oh, that's fine," Sihad says. "We don't need you to apply it to our interests. That's our job. Let's have a look at what you've been working on."

Paul projects his work onto the screen for everyone to see. "Can I get some coffee?" he asks Kyle.

"Of course, where are my manners?" Kyle sends a text off to someone in the office.

The men continue going over Paul's presentation. A few minutes later, coffee and scones arrive.

Paul can't stop shaking from anger and a deep feeling of betrayal. *Several months of my work being handed over for something I don't believe in. And the worst part is that I feel pushed into it, without my consent.*

As time moves into the second hour, Paul excuses himself to use the bathroom. When he is in the bathroom, he texts Collin: *Your suspicions were right. DOD showed up today. Talk later. So mad!* He walks out of the stall and over to the sink to splash water on his face and wash his hands. Two men walk in, talking, ignoring him.

"...and that wasn't the end of it," one of the men says. "They threatened the old guy if he didn't hand over more of the software."

The other man shushes the one talking and nods toward Paul, who pretends to be preoccupied. Looking into the mirror, Paul opens his mouth to inspect his teeth for food.

"I think Christensen is in over his head," the talky man whispers to the other one.

Maybe Kyle is a victim in this as well, Paul thinks to himself. He reaches for the paper-towel dispenser, pulls out enough paper to dry his hands, then heads back to the meeting.

THE FOURSOME STEPS OFF the bus in the small town of Barton. "We're heading over to Nancy's Used Clothing Store if you guys want to come," Sharina says, walking backward and looking at Mora and Aaron.

"Sure," Mora says. "If that's okay with the two of you?"

The four walk along the lightly snow-covered road to the large, red barn structure on the left. When they step inside, a musty smell hits everyone's nostrils. Sharina turns to Chana. "You okay with the smell?" she asks, knowing Chana has been experiencing certain odors as overpowering during her pregnancy.

But Chana is already heading upstairs to the clothing area. "I haven't been shopping in at least a month," Chana says, smiling. Rows of racks with well-organized, used clothing cover the second floor of the barn.

"I could use a new sweater for winter, too," Aaron says as he heads over to the "masculine" clothing section on the left side of the store.

The women sift through the racks, pushing the heavy clothes aside to look at new items. Sharina finds some yoga pants that expand at the waist, along with several other articles of clothing. She hauls them all back to the dressing room to try on. Her black braid swings as she pulls the curtain shut.

"Let me see those on you before you take them off," Chana says through the curtain. Then Chana pulls the curtain next to Sharina's and tries on a couple of sweaters.

"Here," Sharina says, standing outside of Chana's dressing room drape. Chana pulls the drape aside and laughs. Sharina is wearing a pair of red, one-piece, long underwear with a drop seat. "I don't even have to take them off when I give birth," Sharina says. "I can just drop the seat fly and stay warm."

Chana laughs.

Mora is holding up sweaters she thinks Aaron might like, and Aaron is alternately nodding "Yes" or shaking his head "No" from across the isle. Aaron is wearing a tall, green-and-white-striped hat that looks like something from a Dr. Seuss book.

Everyone finds something to laugh about, and the four of them feel their friendship deepening.

After an hour of trying on clothes, Mora calls over to Sharina and Chana. "We'll meet you guys downstairs at the checkout." She and Aaron head downstairs.

By this time, other people are roaming around the upper floor, looking at clothes. One of them quickly moves over to where Chana is pushing the rack of clothes to one side. Suddenly she feels something hard in her side and hears words whispered in her ear.

"If you move," the voice says, "I will shoot you and then your friend. I know who you are, and you'll be okay if you just do as I say. Keep looking at the clothes. Don't turn around."

Chana's heart begins to race. She looks up to see Sharina, who is in the next aisle, about ten feet away. When Sharina looks up at Chana, she notices a man standing very close to her, and then she sees Chana's face.

"Look at this one," Sharina says, as if joking as she walks over to Chana.

"Don't blow it!" the man whispers to Chana as Sharina comes closer. Quickly, Sharina reaches for Chana's hand across the rack of clothes. The room freezes as their hands meld into a glowing gold color.

"You okay?" Sharina looks at Chana, who is crying.

"Yes. Is he frozen?" Chana begins to ask, when Aaron appears at the top of the stairs. In a few large steps, Aaron is next to the young women and he grabs them by their arms. When he touches them, an unfamiliar feeling of power washes over him. He is seeing their world from the inside and looking out.

Finally, he manages to compose himself. "You guys okay?" he asks, looking at the man holding his gun in a frozen position.

"Yes, we're okay," Sharina replies. Let's get out of here." The three start to head for the door. "Wait," Chana says. Still holding on to Sharina, she walks back toward the man. She takes the gun from his hand and grabs the red longjohns from Sharina's hand. She puts them in the man's hand, keeping the gun. "Okay," she says. "Let's go!"

The three come to the top of the stairs, where they can see Mora moving around at the bottom.

"Come on, you guys!" Mora says. "We need to get out of here!"

As everyone heads for the door, Chana drops forty dollars on the counter. "That should cover it," she says to the frozen clerk behind the till, and they all dash out the door. Outside, the people who had been frozen on the sidewalks have resumed moving.

"This way," Aaron says, knowing everyone inside will start moving again soon.

They all sneak behind the barn and through a field to the street on another block.

"Here," Aaron says to them, directing them toward an old, deserted school bus. "Get in!"

Everyone gets into the bus and crouches down low, sitting on the floor.

"Who was that man?" a visibly shaken Chana asks Sharina.

"I've seen him before," Sharina says. "In front of my apartment, back home."

"Shhhh!" Aaron hushes the young women, and Mora embraces them from behind.

Everyone sits in silence, listening. After a few minutes pass, their heads start to pop up, taking a peek out the windows.

"I think he's gone," Sharina says to Aaron. "That was too close!" she adds, looking at the others.

Aaron is the first to step outside the bus. He looks in all directions but doesn't see anything unusual. More importantly, he doesn't sense anything threatening.

Sharina texts Teylen, knowing her mom experiences it when she uses her special ability: *We're okay. No need to worry. Explain when we get home.*

"Let's treat ourselves to a ride," Aaron says. He walks out to the road and hails a pickup truck coming toward them. The driver pulls over about thirty feet down the road. "Come on!" Aaron yells back at the others.

Everyone walks toward the stopped vehicle. Reaching the passenger side of the truck first, Aaron opens the door and asks the driver, "Can you give us a lift to the end of Songthrush Road, up ahead?"

The driver turns his head to view the three women walking toward the truck and then looks back at Aaron. "Sure," he says. "You can all ride in the back."

Aaron notices that the truck's front seat and floor are full of work gear. "Thank you so much," he says as he motions toward the women to hurry up. Aaron drops the truck's tailgate and watches the middle-aged man seated behind the steering wheel as the women climb in and situate themselves. Mora is still comforting Chana, who is visibly shaken. Sharina moves closer to Chana in the back of the truck and puts her arm around her. Aaron waves to the driver, who pulls back out into traffic.

Everyone gathers close as the truck bumps along the rural road. Sharina places her hand on Chana's belly, then picks up Chana's hand and places it on her own. The whole group is suddenly encased in a golden glow of warmth. The bumpiness of the ride ceases temporarily, as if the truck is suspended a few inches off the ground.

Silent smiles are exchanged as the truck moves through the brisk afternoon air. Chana begins to relax. "That's amazing!" she says to Sharina.

"I know," Sharina says, her eyes creasing at the corners as she smiles back at Chana. "The babies are gaining in power!"

FROM OUTSIDE, THE APARTMENT looks strangely lost with no one living in it, Paul thinks. He stays seated in the park across the street for an hour, pretending to read a paper. He keeps looking over the top of the paper toward his building, to see if anyone is watching it or following him. The sun is starting to set as evening begins to cover Portland in layers of lavender. Paul is tired from the flights of travel.

Finally he gets up, walks across the street, and pushes the coded buttons that open the large, glass doors. As he is standing in the lobby, a wave of loss and memories washes over him. The first time he and Sharina saw this place, they had quickly agreed they liked it, and then moved in together a few weeks later. They were so excited to finally land the apartment, after months of hunting in vain.

Smiling at the memory, Paul walks toward the stairs and heads up. The hallway to their apartment door looks empty, but otherwise the same as always. As he wanders down the hall to his apartment door, more memories flood his mind. He unlocks the door, pushes it open, and stands outside, looking in. More memories.

Stepping inside, his stomach leaps to his throat. The place looks untouched, except for a message scrawled across the kitchen cabinets: "WHERE IS THE FREAK?" Suddenly, Paul realizes the man who had been watching their apartment was about Sharina, not him.

He reaches for his phone and dials Teylen's landline, not wanting to scare Sharina. "Teylen, hello, this is Paul. Yes, I need to know, where is Sharina?" Pause. "She's not back yet?" Pause. "I am worried. Someone broke into our apartment, and it is clear they are looking for her." Pause. "I'm glad she let you know they were okay. Will you have her call me as soon as she gets back? I need to let her know someone is looking for her. And Teylen, be careful." Long pause, then, "I'm coming home tonight on a red eye. Won't make it back until tomorrow morning, though." Another pause. "I will, Teylen. Don't worry."

As Paul hangs up his burner phone, he turns to see someone dart past the apartment door. He runs into the hallway to catch the stairway door closing. He runs back into his apartment and looks out the window and down at the street. A minute later, the front door to the building opens and someone dressed in a suit walks out onto the street and gets into the passenger side of a black SUV that is waiting for him. As the vehicle drives off, Paul sees that it has a government plate.

Paul drops to his knees beside the couch, his insides shaken. *What have I done?* "I know I have no right to claim her as mine." He lifts his head upward into the empty apartment, unsure of where the words are coming from. "Just keep her safe, and I will always watch out for her. I'll do whatever is needed." He hesitates before his next words, never having been a religious man. "Please make me worthy." He drops his head into his hands, allowing tears of stress to run down his arms and fall into the cracks of the couch.

W HEN THE TRUCK DRIVER PULLS OVER to drop them all
off at the end of a road that isn't theirs, Aaron jumps
out and opens the passenger door to talk to the driver.
"Thank you so much," he says, then pulls out a fifty-dollar bill.
"This is for your trouble, but also for your memory of ever having
seen us."

The truck driver looks back at the three women sliding off the
tailgate. He notices just how young two of them are and how
scared one of them appears. Sticking his head out the window, he
calls back to them, "Are you guys okay?"

Sharina walks over to the driver's window. "Thank you for the
ride," she says as she places her hand on the man's arm and smiles
at him. As their eyes meet, the man suddenly realizes his chronic
back pain has disappeared. He feels electricity running through
his body.

"That's amazing," he says to Sharina. Then he asks, as if he'd
never seen her before, "Do you guys need a ride into town?"

Realizing that the man now has no memory of the previous
ride, she replies, "Thank you for offering, but we're just headed

down the road a bit." She steps back from the truck and stands with Aaron and the others.

The truck driver pulls back out into traffic and waves at the group of young people as they continue to walk toward their road, another quarter-mile away.

"Wow," Aaron jokes as they start to walk, "you saved me fifty bucks. Thanks!"

"Darn!" Chana says as they are walking.

"What?" Mora asks.

"I forgot to get G'ma Luani's hand lotion!"

"Under the circumstances, I'm pretty sure she'll forgive you, Chana. It isn't every day you have someone stick a gun in your back!"

Chana tries to smile at Mora. "I know. I just hate disappointing my g'ma." Everyone is silent as they continue walking.

Reaching the beginning of Teylen's farm road, they make the turn off the pavement and onto the dirt, where the dusting of snow is thickening. "What are you thinking about?" Sharina asks Aaron as they are walking.

Aaron looks up at her. Everyone is looking at him. "I'm not going to say," Aaron replies, a little embarrassed.

"Why?" Mora asks. "What are you thinking about?"

Aaron starts to blush. "Well, if you have to know, I was thinking about those chicken pot pies that Minki, June, and Luani were making, and how hungry I am."

Everyone laughs.

"Me, too!" Sharina says with a smile, and she places a protective arm around Chana's shoulders. "Let's let go of today and enjoy our group dinner tonight. I need some laughs and relaxation after the day we've had. And Paul may make it back in time…I can't wait to see him!"

"Do you ever notice that you're tired after we create the disturbance?" Chana asks Sharina, solemnly placing her hands in her pockets.

Sharina thinks for a moment. "Yes, but I'm not sure what it is that makes me tired. Sometimes it seems like it's the stress of the situation and not the actual action that we're creating. I can't tell yet. But yes, I'm tired. Could just be from being pregnant." She keeps walking toward the farm houses that are becoming visible, off in the distance.

"I'm so glad Mora and I are a part of whatever this is," Aaron says, "and I'm glad we were there today. Thanks for letting us tag along." He looks at Mora, who smiles and nods her head.

"Me, too," Chana says. "I always feel better with you two around."

The four hold hands and continue walking down the road, a flickering gold hue hovering above them. Suddenly Sharina breaks rank and runs out ahead, doing a backward, crazy-lady dance.

"Chicken pot piiiieees!" she says emphatically toward her friends, smiling and dancing from one foot to the other.

Chana laughs.

TEYLEN, MINKI, JUNE, AND GRANDMA LUANI all have flour on their aprons as they finish laying the top crusts on the pies. Grandma Luani is sitting down, resting and having tea while the others finish up. She catches a look on Teylen's face and realizes Teylen is shaking.

"You are not feeling well," G'ma Luani says to Teylen. "You should go lie down."

The other women look at Teylen, who has stopped working on the pies. Flour is stuck to her hands, which hang down by her sides.

"Teylen, can you hear me?" Minki moves closer, but Teylen doesn't move. "Tey!" she yells, but nothing.

A few seconds later, Teylen relaxes and looks up to see everyone staring at her. "Something has happened to make the daughters use their ability," she says.

June takes Teylen's flour-covered right hand and moves her to a chair. "Here, sit down," June says. "What has happened? Please tell me."

Teylen shakes her head. "I'm not sure, but they had to use their ability. I can sense that they are okay now. It's okay, June." June sits down next to her. Teylen's burner phone bings, and everyone looks at her pocket. Dusting her hands off, she reaches for the phone. "It's Sharina. She says everyone is okay and she'll explain when they get home. Can't come home yet but will be home by four. They're okay, June. See?" Teylen passes the phone to June, and June handles it carefully.

"What do you think happened?" June asks.

"I don't know, but we'll find out when they get here. Let's keep working on these and get dinner ready. I'm sure everyone will be hungry when they hit the farm." Teylen walks over to the sink and washes her hands, whispering a spirit prayer as she does so, not wanting June to see her worry.

***

Huang and June are moving another table into place in Lisa's long dining room. The women had agreed that they'd prepare dinner at Minki's farm but eat at Lisa's, since she had a room big enough to accommodate all of them. Huang unfolds the legs from under the long, portable table he had brought in from the storage shed. "I need to get a rag and clean off some of the cobwebs," he says to June, and starts walking toward the mudroom.

"I'll get it," June says, and makes her way to the mudroom, off the kitchen. Just then the mudroom door pops open, and Chana walks in with Mora and Aaron. June looks up. "Oh, thank God!" she says, and she reaches for her daughter and pulls her close.

"It's okay, June. Everyone is okay," Mora says.

"Teylen came over to Minki's while we were baking and received a text from Sharina," June tells Mora.

"Oh good, you're back!" Huang comes into the mudroom to hug his daughter.

"You guys, I'm okay," Chana says. "I came over here because Minki said you were here and I knew you'd be worrying. Everything is fine. Mora and Aaron took good care of us, and we even got some new, old clothes." Chana holds up four clothing items for June and Huang to see.

"So, success!" Huang says, trying to downplay the seriousness of what had happened. Lisa walks into the kitchen and begins to pull the pies from the oven. She had baked two of them there, and Minki had baked two of them in her oven.

"Come on, you guys," Lisa yells from the kitchen. "Let's get the tables set up. Everyone will be here soon!"

"That's me," Huang tells Chana. "I'm on table setup."

"I'll come help you, Dad," Chana says. "I'll just leave these clothes here by the door, if that's okay with Lisa." She looks up at Lisa.

"Chana, could you put those on the back bed so no one trips on them?" Lisa suggests as she pulls out the last pie. Chana heads down the hall to the back room. June follows her into the room.

"Teylen said someone tried to grab you or something. What happened?" June sits down on the bed and looks up at Chana.

"Mom, let's try to enjoy our dinner. I'm fine. I'm not sure what the man wanted. Sharina and Aaron had everything under control. We were not in danger." Chana beams her biggest smile at her mom and sits down next to her on the bed. She can feel the white chenille spread pressing its pattern into the back of her legs. She leans over and hugs her mother. "Please. Let's talk about it later?" Chana's face pleads with her mom. "I'm super hungry."

"Okay. But we will talk about it later!" June says. The two get up and walk out of the bedroom. "I think Lisa has some bananas and crackers in the kitchen. Maybe that will help until we eat?"

D R. PORTER MISSED HER RESEARCH COLLEAGUE being in the office. Huang was bright and caught on quickly to patterns, something that was quite useful in their research. But the two had also become friends, and Carol Porter was aware that her office felt very lonely without him. She walks over to his desk and thinks about bringing in another researcher to cover the hands-on part of their research. Huang could continue to work from wherever he was. Dr. Porter had agreed with Huang that it was best she not know where he was. Since the move, his work was coming through an anonymous router, and they were able to keep up on their research this way. But Huang had indicated he was making different plans for his family's future, and being a researcher wasn't part of his plan.

Deep in thought about her future employee needs, Dr. Porter feels a hand reach from behind her and cover her mouth.

"Don't scream, and I will let you go," a voice says.

Dr. Porter bites the man's hand, right through his glove.

"Ow, you bitch!" the man exclaims. "Why did you do that?!"

Porter picks up a scalpel lying on the testing table and points it toward the intruder. "Who are you, and what do you want?"

The man is still shaking his hand.

"Where's Huang Li?" the man says, brow stitched in pain.

"Okay, now the 'who are you' part!" Dr. Porter says.

"Let's suffice it to say I work for the Feds." The man pulls out his wallet and shows her an I.D.

"Sean Webb…Department of Defense…Investigative Branch? Wow," Carol says, looking up at the man. "And why does the DOD have an interest in our small research lab, Mr. Webb?"

Webb takes off his glove and examines his hand. "You bit me all the way through my glove!" he says, showing her the teeth marks in his hand.

"Yeah, and you scared me when you sneaked into my lab and came up behind me and covered my mouth. So we're even. In fact, I think I still owe you a little more pain, so you'd better level with me, Mr. Webb. What do you want here?"

"Where's your assistant, Mr. Li?" The man sucks on the bite mark and shakes his hand some more.

"Huang? You're here looking for Huang?" Dr. Porter lowers the scalpel. "He's on vacation with his family. I don't know where they went. He has a well-earned month off. What do you want with Huang Li?" She raises the scalpel again, pointing it at Webb. Webb looks around the research lab and over to Mr. Li's work area, behind Carol. His eyes light on a family photo of Li, June, and Chana. Dr. Porter follows his eyes to the propped-up photograph. "Oh, so perhaps it's not Huang you're looking for after all?"

"I'm not at liberty to discuss our investigation with you," Webb says. "I just need to locate Mr. Huang Li. Do you know where he's vacationing?"

"No, I already told you I don't know!" Dr. Porter says angrily. "Maybe he's just home and decided to have a staycation? Did you check his home?"

Webb mumbles something to himself. "Here's my card." He hands Dr. Porter a card with his phone number and email address. "Please have him contact us as soon as you hear from him?" Webb gets up to leave.

"Wait a minute!" Dr. Porter walks toward the door and shuts it. She places herself between the door and Webb. "What gives you the right to sneak into my lab and grab me from behind, Mr. Webb? If you had just knocked on my door and asked about Mr. Li, I could have told you the same information you have now." Dr. Porter reaches behind her and locks the lab door.

"Look, Lady, you don't want to do this." Webb starts to reach inside his coat, and Dr. Porter brings the scalpel right up to the man's neck.

"You know, there are two things in the world that really piss me off, and one of them is when stupid men like yourself call me 'lady.' You have now called me 'bitch' and 'lady.'"

Webb's hands are up in the air. Dr. Porter reaches inside his coat and pulls out his gun from its holster.

"Well, looky here," she says, holding the gun up in front of the man. Then she sets the scalpel down and holds the gun on Webb. Looking down quickly at it, she sees the safety is on and she surreptitiously flicks it off.

"And what's the other thing?" Webb asks.

"What?" Dr. Porter looks at Webb as if he is crazy.

"What's the other thing that makes you mad?" Webb repeats.

"Oh, right. Well, the other thing is when people break into my lab and steal my stuff. Recently a folder went missing from my file cabinet, and I noticed that someone had tried to bypass the security features. You wouldn't know anything about that, would you?"

Webb slowly lowers his arms.

"I didn't say you could do that." Dr. Porter pushes the gun toward him. His arms go back up. "What do you want with Huang's family?" she asks.

Webb stands still, looking out the window.

"Did I tell you that I was raised with a father who was a sharp-shooter for the U.S. Olympics team?" Dr. Porter says. "My dad knew everything about guns." She pauses. "You see this gun here?" She raises the gun in her hand. "This is a gun someone issues you. It is a gun used by federal agents and police. A good gun, but not really impressive. It is a gun for someone who does what he is told and doesn't really think for himself. A follower. Is that you, Mr. Webb? Are you a follower who can't think for yourself?"

"I'm trying to locate his daughter," Webb blurts out.

"Why?" Dr. Porter asks. Webb stands still, eyes wandering outside the window. Dr. Porter moves closer. "Tell me what you want with Chana Li, and maybe I'll let you live." She motions for the man to sit down in the chair that is next to where he is standing.

"It's a long story and I don't know all of it," Webb begins. "I just know that they want her. I'm supposed to locate her and bring her in. I'm not really happy about having to locate an eighteen-year-old to bring to my superiors," Webb says, looking down at the ugly, green flooring.

"What do they want with her?" Dr. Porter replies.

"I'm not sure. I just know that she and another young woman are in their sights and I'm suppose to deliver both of them by Friday."

"This Friday? That's only two days from now." Dr. Porter looks at the calendar to their right.

"Yes!" says Webb.

Dr. Porter sits and thinks. She can't let him go. She needs to keep him somewhere so he can't communicate with his superiors.

She gets closer to the man and rubs her left hand over his pocket. "Stand up!" she says, and steps back from him. She reaches into his pocket and pulls out his phone, then pockets it. "Put that lab coat on, over there." Dr. Porter motions to a lab coat hanging on the back of a chair.

Webb stands up and walks over to the lab coat. "Really, La—" he stops himself. "Really, Dr. Porter. Is this necessary?"

"Yes, really, Mr. Webb. This is necessary because you came here uninvited and broke into my lab. I am just defending myself until I can call the proper authorities."

Webb slips the lab coat on.

"Now, you're going to tape your mouth with that duct tape, right there," she nods to the tape roll.

After Webb has his mouth properly covered, Porter has him sit down and she secures his hands behind him with a piece of rope. Then she ties his legs so he can walk, but not run. "You'll have to take small steps," she says. "We're headed to my car. First car to the right of the front door. Let's see," she looks at her watch. "It's five-forty-five. We'll wait a few more minutes for the parking lot to clear out, and then we'll go."

At six-fifteen, the two slowly walk from the lab down to the front door of the building. Dr. Porter opens the car door on the passenger side, having left Huang's Jeep in her garage. "Sit down!" she demands. Webb sits, and Dr. Porter lowers the gun and swings his legs into the car. She seatbelts him tightly into his seat. His eyes are looking around her car. There is little to give him any clues into the doctor's life. She shuts the car door and walks to the other side. Before getting in, she makes a call. Webb can hear her talking outside the car, but he can't make out what is being said. The door opens and she gets in.

"I believe you're staying with me, Mr. Webb, until we can find you some long-term accommodations. Hope you like cats!" Dr. Porter starts up the car.

E VERYONE LISTENS AS SHARINA gives her account of the used-clothing store incident. "I look up at Chana and there is this man getting closer to her…so I kept my eye on her and moved closer like I was still looking at the clothes. By the time he was next to her, I was able to touch Chana from across the rack of clothes. We just held hands and, well, you know how it goes."

June turns to Huang with a look of concern. Everyone is talking to each other.

"So, they want you," says G'ma Luani's voice out loud. The talking stops.

"Luani is right," Collin says. "They want both of you, or they wouldn't have tried that in public, during the day."

"But why would they want the young women?" Minki says. "How would they know about them, and what could they possibly want with them? It's not as if they know something. They don't even completely understand these pregnancies. Shoot, *we* don't even completely understand what is happening here!"

Teylen reaches over and puts her arm around her friend. "We all need to stay calm and continue taking care of ourselves," she says.

The table is a sea of dishes, silverware, and glasses. The pies are almost completely gone. Teylen pulls her pipe out of her pocket and walks over to the window and opens it a crack. She lights the contents of her pipe, takes a puff, and blows the smoke out the window. After a few more puffs, she snuffs it out and says to the group, "Come on, you guys. Let's head outside and light the fire."

Everyone gets up from the table and pushes their chairs in.

"I'm staying in to do dishes," Collin says. "I didn't get the outside work done today because of my office work, so let me do dishes to be part of this?"

Lisa nods. Everyone picks up their plates and heads out to the kitchen.

"I'm going to help Collin," Sharina says. "You guys go out and get the fire going and we'll be right out." She smiles at Lisa and gives Minki a hug. "Go on. We're fine in here."

The others grab up coats and slip feet into boots. Heads are being covered with hats as the group moves outside to the fire ring. Teylen makes her way back to the refrigerator, reaches inside, and pulls out two beers. Setting one down, she opens the other one and sets it on the window sill above the kitchen sink.

"For you," she says, nodding at Collin. "None for her," she says, pointing to Sharina.

"I don't drink, Mom. You know that." Sharina continues to haul used dinner glasses from the dining room into the kitchen.

"Just thought I'd be sure…you know, the baby and all." Teylen smiles at Sharina. "I'll be outside waiting for you guys."

The two stand before the sink with the dishwasher open, Collin rinsing the dinnerware and Sharina putting it into the dishwasher.

"So, how's your work going, Collin?" Sharina asks. "Are you able to keep up with the DOD's demands while you're out here?" She reaches for the next plate.

"It's not easy, but that satellite connection is working great. I'll probably need to go in for a meeting in a few weeks to appease everyone." He hands Sharina another plate and she slips it in between the dishwasher's holding prongs. "How about you? I suppose your job being 'in person' makes it impossible to do from here."

"I've been Skyping classes for people who want yoga from home. I did have to hand my classes over for a while, but I'm able to keep up with all the teachers and see what they're doing. Most of my job is being supportive of other yoga and fitness instructors and managing their schedules. I can pretty much do all of that from here."

Collin hands her another plate.

"Hey, are you comfortable, staying at Lisa's with Mora and Aaron?" Sharina asks.

"Oh yeah, it's working out just fine. I love getting out in the early morning and getting work done for Lisa. Your mom and her friends have been unbelievably accommodating about all of this. And the basement computer room at Teylen's has really come together. It's been great for me here." Collin smiles and bounces his head in affirmation. "I'm just worried that we're asking a lot of Teylen and Minki and Lisa to suddenly take us all in."

"Teylen wouldn't want to be anywhere else," Sharina replies. "She's thrilled we're all here. And the money everyone is giving her for food and rent is helping her. It's okay. Don't worry about Mom. She loves having people around the farm. So do Minki and Lisa."

Collin hands Sharina the last plate and washes the soap off his hands.

Sharina surveys the dishwasher. "I don't think we can get one more thing in there. Why don't you take that beer and head out? I'm going to tidy up the dining room just a little bit more." As Sharina walks back to the dining room, Collin pulls out his laptop and sits down at the kitchen table for a minute. "You're going to do work now?" Sharina asks him incredulously, hands full of folding chairs.

"I just wanted to check some of the work I was looking at earlier with Paul. I have this array of code that just isn't making sense. I get it all written and then it doesn't work right…" Collin's head is down as he pores over the computer. Sharina lays the chairs up against the wall, near the back door, to be taken out to the shed later on. Then she heads back through the kitchen to the dining room.

"Wait a minute!" Collin says. "Do that again."

"Do what again?" Sharina is halfway to the dining room, looking back at Collin in the kitchen.

"Walk through the kitchen again, will you, Sha?" Collin watches his array as Sharina walks back through the middle of the kitchen, past his array so neatly laid out on his screen. When she walks through, a disruption happens on the screen. The computer attempts to hold the array, reconfigures into something unrecognizable, and then returns to its original configuration on the screen. "Well, I guess that explains that!" Collin says, looking at Sharina.

"That explains what?" Sharina says from across the room. Slowly she heads over toward Collin's computer. The array shakes again, and evidence of static appears on the screen. Sharina looks down at the screen and sees it. She places her hand over her mouth.

"Yeah," Collin says. "Pretty unbelievable! And look: This page I've been working on that doesn't have anything to do with the vibrational weaponry, it isn't affected when you walk by. It's fine.

Just the coding pages that have to do with the suspected weaponry."

"And the baby is just finishing its first trimester," Sharina says.
"I wonder if it'll get stronger the further along it gets?"

Sharina and Collin's eyes meet.

"This explains why I couldn't get the array to hold when I tried
to save it," Collin says. "I knew the algorithms were complex, but
what I was seeing was extraordinary…I'd never seen anything like
it before. It would explain why they'd come after you guys." He
looks up at Sharina with deep concern.

"And maybe it answers your questions about exactly what it is
you're working on?" Sharina puts her hand on Collin's hand and
presses down. "And what Paul is working on…" she says, looking
up, wishing he had returned home by now.

PAUL'S PHONE RINGS. It's Huang. "Huang, is everything okay?" Paul's voice is quick with concern.

"I just got a call from my boss, Dr. Porter. She says an agent of some type broke into her lab and tried to subdue her. He was looking for information on Sharina and Chana."

"Is Dr. Porter okay? What happened?"

"Yes, my boss is fine. She has the man in her house in Portland and she's holding him hostage."

"What?! Why is she doing that?!"

"Think about it, Paul. He's trying to get information about Sharina and Chana. They'll just keep coming. I'm with Dr. Porter; I think we need to reprogram this guy and get him on our side. Then we can send him back in and find out what this is."

"We could go to prison, Huang." Paul bites his lower lip.

"Aren't we kind of already there?" Huang replies.

There is a moment of silence. Paul thinks about the words scrawled across the apartment's kitchen cabinet doors. Then Paul says, "Give me her address. Oh, and Huang, buy me a ticket for this guy to get him back to Vermont?"

"How will you keep him from talking while you're flying?" Huang asks.

"I'll tell him I'm taking him to meet the women. That's what he wants, right? Oh, and Huang? Please tell Sharina I'm okay. She texted me and said something about understanding why they're interested in her and Chana. Tell her we'll talk when I get back there, and explain why I'm a day late?"

"I will, Paul, and I'll get that ticket. Send me this guy's name and DOB when you know it."

D R. PORTER OPENS THE DOOR only an inch. "I'm Paul," announces a voice on the other side. "Huang sent me."
Dr. Porter speaks through the open crack. "What's your wife's name?"

"Sharina." Paul smiles at Dr. Porter. "It's nice to meet you in person finally."

The door opens wide and Carol Porter invites Paul inside. Seated on her couch is a man with his hands tied and his mouth covered.

"Is that really necessary?" Paul asks Dr. Porter.

"It is until I can be assured he won't scream."

Paul walks over to the man on the couch.

"Hi, I'm Paul...Sharina Mathews' boyfriend. You were looking for information about her and Chana Li?" The man on the couch nods.

"How about I just take you to them, and you can meet them in person? Would that be okay?"

The man nods vigorously.

"I'm going to remove this tape on your mouth, but you have to promise not to scream or the deal's off. Understand?"

The man nods a third time.

Paul carefully loosens the tape and removes it. "Dr. Porter, will you get us some type of lotion for our friend's face?"

Dr. Porter walks out of the living room and into the back room, returning with the face cream.

"Could I have some water, please?" Mr. Webb asks.

Dr. Porter walks into her kitchen and brings Sean Webb a glass of water and sets it on a coaster on the coffee table, in front of him.

"I want you to know that Dr. Porter is only protecting Sharina and Chana," Paul says to the man. "She never intended to hurt you, and you did break into her lab and threatened her."

"I'm just doing my job," the man replies. "I was told to keep Dr. Porter under surveillance and follow Huang Li to his home and…uh…"

"And uh what?" Paul asks. "I don't think your bosses have thought this through. These are young women who haven't done anything wrong. You can't just bring them in. You would have to charge them with something."

"I'm not police," the man says, looking up at Porter. "I work for the Feds. And believe me, they can do whatever they want."

"And may I ask your name?" Paul says.

"His name is allegedly Sean Webb," Dr. Porter says, holding up the ID card she had taken off of him. "And he works for the DOD, Investigative Branch."

Paul turns to Webb. "The DOD!? What does the DOD want with a couple of young women?"

"My job is to find out as much as I can and report back to them. I wasn't going to hurt anyone."

"You were prepared to shoot me!" Dr. Porter yells.

"I'm sorry. You surprised me that you were still in the lab. I thought no one was there. I didn't draw my gun. You did that."

"Somehow that doesn't make me feel any better!" Dr. Porter says as she sits down across from Webb.

"Okay, Sean, here's what we're going to do." Paul shifts around on the couch to face Sean Webb directly. "I'm going to untie you and let you get out of this lab coat. Then you and I are going on a little trip, but you can't have your phone, nor can you communicate with anyone in any other way…or the deal is off and you don't meet them."

"I don't know…" Webb starts to speak.

"Sean! I thought you wanted information on these women? I think meeting them counts as information, and I'm offering you a meetup. No one is going to hurt you. No harm will come to you. I give you my word." Paul puts his hand up in the air as if swearing an oath.

"Where are they?" Webb asks.

"Patience!" Paul admonishes him.

Dr. Porter places the face cream on the coffee table in front of Webb. "I'm sorry I taped your face," she says as she sets it down.

"I need to use a restroom." Webb looks at Paul.

"And I need your word, 'Sean Webb,' that you will come peacefully with me and you will not communicate with your superiors until you have met the women." Paul looks sternly into Webb's face. Webb has a square jaw and a day of beard growth, which is dark against his pale skin. Paul guesses Webb's age to be about forty.

"I give you my word," Webb says. "But I get to meet them, and talk to them."

"That's right," Paul says. "So we are all agreed. I can cut this rope off you, and you will be fair to us as we are being fair to you."

"Yes, we're agreed," Webb reiterates, squirming slightly.

Paul pulls out his pocket knife and cuts the rope around Mr. Webb's ankles. "Lean forward, Sean." Paul cuts the rope off his wrists.

"May I use your restroom, please?" Webb asks Dr. Porter as he picks up the face cream and heads across the room.

"Yes, you may. Please use the guest towel," she yells after him as he heads to the bathroom.

"And leave the door open so we can hear you," Paul says as Webb steps inside.

Paul's phone vibrates in his back pocket. It's a text from Huang. *Need a name for this ticket!*

Mr. Sean Webb, Paul texts back. *DOB 9-18-69.*

T HE MORNING YOGA CLASS in Teylen's barn had initially begun with just Sharina and Chana. The next day, Mora had decided that a morning stretch/workout would do her well, so she joined. A few days later, Aaron felt he could also benefit from the workout and he began to show up. Within two weeks, everyone was up and going through some morning meditations and yoga in Teylen's barn.

Sharina encourages everyone to walk first, then bend, then stretch, and finally work on strength via a variety of more-or-less traditional yoga poses, or asanas. She leads them through a series of asanas, each flowing into the next, gradually guiding them back into their bodies, their opened minds, their breath. The older people move through the beginning poses, then head home to get fires going and some tea on. Aaron sometimes stays behind to use a couple pieces of workout equipment Teylen had stored in her barn.

Everyone seems to be more settled since Sharina had started teaching yoga in the barn. As they lie in shavasana, also known as "corpse pose," Sharina speaks to them. "We are all one and connected to every other living thing. How we treat the tree is how we treat ourself. Much of the world has lost sight of this connection and they are adrift, desiring the connection and trying to find it in ways that do not satisfy. As we lie here with our open minds, may we allow every living thing into our hearts to be owned by our love as we love ourself."

Then there is a long silence and no one moves. Just breathes.

"When you're ready," Sharina continues, "roll to the left or right and sit up and take a seat." She sits to face her ad hoc class. June and Chana are up close; Aaron and Mora are next to them; Huang and Collin are behind. The morning light is just starting to come through the barn's windows. "Namasté," Sharina says.

Everyone gets up, rolls their mats, and heads out of the barn. Collin, Mora, and Aaron wave as they head down the road toward Lisa's farm. Huang and June head next door, and Chana stays behind to have breakfast with Sharina and Teylen this morning.

"What time did Paul say he would be coming in to the Burlington airport?" Chana asks Sharina, knowing she has been missing him.

"He's supposed to hit the airport around two today, so they should be arriving here by four-thirty," Sharina replies. "Are you nervous about meeting the DOD guy?" Sharina's hair is piled up on top of her head, with a hat pulled down around her ears. Her breath comes in clouds of warmth in the cold December morning air.

"A little," Chana replies. "But I trust Paul and Dr. Porter. Do you trust Paul and Dr. Porter?"

"Yes, you know I do. What's going on, Chana?" Sharina stops to look at her sweetest friend. Chana is a beautiful young woman. She has curiosity in her eyes, which slant downward at the ends and look deeply into Sharina's eyes when they meet. She is shorter than Sharina, but not by much. She is keeping her hair short with a blunt cut that she can do herself in the bathroom, and this morning the straight ends stick out at the sides from under her hat. She reminds Sharina of an Asian warrior princess.

"I guess I am a little nervous about Paul bringing a stranger here. Especially someone who was trying to spy on us." The two women push the barn door shut and continue walking toward the house. The sun has just broken over the hills to the east, and the ground has a new, light dusting of snow. It is a beautiful morning, as if the world is new. The two women's feet make crunching sounds as they walk in step with each other.

"It's okay to be nervous, Chana. I think the best way for the man who is spying on us to become neutralized is to let him get to know us, and Paul agrees. What do you think could go wrong?"

"Maybe he'll be wearing a tracker, and a lot of other people will come and they'll find where we are?" Chana says. "Or maybe he carries some secret poison that he'll slip into our water. I don't know. I'm just feeling a little worried."

Sharina looks at Chana and can see the stress on her face. "We will listen to your worry and proceed with caution. Let's go get some breakfast in us, and then we'll feel more grounded. Teylen's making hashbrowns, and I'm on fruit smoothies this morning." Sharina grabs up Chana's hand and holds it close to her heart.

The two young women stand just outside Teylen's house. They grasp each other's hands and close their eyes. Their hands begin to glow a golden color, and from the road, no one can tell that their feet are about a quarter inch off the ground as they stand just outside the mudroom door entrance.

E VERYONE IS SITTING AROUND Minki's kitchen table when
Paul enters the house with Sean Webb in tow. The group
had decided this was the best way to introduce him to Sharina and Chana. Minki had made her most delicious au gratin
potatoes, and Teylen had brought fried chicken and a huge salad
for the vegetarians among them. The smells of the house swirl all
around, and the conversation is lively—until Paul walks in with
Webb. Then, everyone is silent.

Teylen stands up and offers Webb a chair next to Collin and
Aaron. Sharina gets up, walks over to Paul, and takes his hand.
She pulls him toward the back room.

"So you're the DOD agent who broke into Dr. Porter's office?"
Huang asks.

"Don't you think we could let the man eat first, Huang? He's
had a very long trip." Teylen looks toward Huang and winks.

"If you'll excuse me," Webb says, "I really need to wash up. Is
there a bathroom I could use?" He stands up, and Minki guides
him to the bathroom off the kitchen.

"You have a lovely home," Webb tells her as they walk toward the bathroom.

"Thank you. You are most welcome here." Minki lightly pushes the bathroom door open and returns to the table.

"So we're just going to let him sit down and break bread with us?" Huang questions Minki and the others. "He was after my daughter's medical information. He broke into Dr. Porter's office. Am I the only one who's worried about this guy?"

"Ah, Huang," Teylen says, placing her hand on top of his arm. "Have you never heard the saying, 'Keep your friends close and your enemies closer'? We have one chance to defuse him and bring him over to our side. Let's offer him honey and not vinegar, eh?" Teylen pats Huang's arm just as Webb returns to the table and sits down.

"I'm sorry if I was rude to you earlier," Huang says to Webb.

"No, I'm sorry. You were right. I broke into your boss's lab and was looking for medical information on your daughter. You have every right to be angry." Webb looks around the table, and his eyes land on Chana. "I guess I owe you an apology, as well. I'm sorry I tried to steal your medical file. I really just wanted to find out what you were about, and keep my superiors happy. It's my job, and for me, it's just a job."

Chana smiles at Webb. "Well, here I am eating fried chicken. What do you think so far?"

Webb smiles and thinks, *Jesus, she's just a child,* as he takes a bite of a thigh and looks up. "Wow! This chicken is delicious. Thank you for inviting me for dinner."

Mora turns to Aaron and starts talking about the job she had applied for at the closest hospital. Sean can hear Aaron saying, "That's an hour and forty-five minute drive one way, Mora. You sure you want to make that drive?" And Lisa is asking Minki about the ingredients in her potatoes.

Chana just stares at Mr. Webb. Every time he looks her way, she raises her eyebrows and holds up her fork, as if she's saying "cheers" to him. Then she looks away and asks Collin how his work on Lisa's farm is coming.

"Well," Collin says, "the winter is quickly coming, but I think I'll have the new roof on the coop by Friday at the latest. There was a setback with the materials I picked up at the hardware store. Got the wrong screws."

"Isn't it great, Minki and Lisa, to have men around doing work on our farms?" Teylen asks her sister farmers. Then she pours a little white wine into a glass in front of her, but stops when she sees that Mr. Webb has none. Handing the bottle to Collin, she says, "Here, Collin, please pour Mr. Webb some wine."

Collin takes the bottle and pours Webb half a glass.

Teylen stands. "To men working on our farms. May the winds just keep bringing more who do not mind getting their hands in the soil." She holds her glass up, and Minki and Lisa also stand.

"To men who work on our farms!" they repeat.

Then everyone takes a sip and begins laughing.

"I have a special job for you, Mr. Webb." Teylen warns her new guest as she sits back down, catching him with his mouth full of potatoes.

Webb swallows. "I'd love to help out while I'm here. I was raised on a farm and love country living."

"Then why did you become a DOD agent?" Chana asks. Everyone gets quiet.

"It seemed like a good opportunity at the time. One I couldn't pass up when they offered me the training and the job. And I guess people change as they age. We start out thinking we want to do one thing, but then we're not the same person twenty years later."

"Isn't that the truth," Aaron says. "I thought I wanted to be a soldier. Now, it's the last thing I would ever put my hand to." He sits quietly, reflecting.

"Being a DOD agent is very rewarding," Webb says. "I get to see lots of the world, and I work with interesting people doing all kinds of interesting things."

"Like killing cats?" Collin asks, without looking toward Mr. Webb.

"I'm not sure I understand," Webb replies, putting his wine glass down and looking at the others for an explanation.

"Oh, don't listen to him," Teylen says. "Someone killed his cat in a cruel way, an unthinkable way. A way that only someone with no heart would do. We can all see that you have a heart, Mr. Webb. You couldn't possibly be the person who killed Collin's cat." Teylen motions toward Collin and continues to eat.

"Someone killed your cat?" Webb asks Collin.

Collin puts his fork down and utters, "Excuse me," then walks away.

"I'm sorry. Did I say something wrong?" Webb asks the group.

"No, Mr. Webb," Chana says, smiling from across the table. "Not yet."

"WE'RE NOT GOING TO HURT THE BABY if we have sex," Sharina says to Paul. "I'm just barely out of my first trimester."

Paul kisses Sharina's forehead. "But we're at Minki's house, in Huang and June's room. Let's wait until we're back at Teylen's?" He hugs Sharina and kisses her some more.

"I just missed you so much, and I miss us," Sharina replies, as she and Paul fall into a large, soft chair in the corner of the room.

"I miss us too, Sharina. What do you think of our Mr. Webb?"

"I can't believe he agreed to come here with you," she replies. "What's the plan?"

"I think the idea is that if he meets you and Chana and sees how ordinary you are, he'll give up and take that information back to his superiors. Teylen seems to think it's best if we make friends with him before he reports back." Paul smiles at his girlfriend's beautiful face.

"I want to make friends with you," Sharina says playfully, biting Paul on his earlobe.

"Sha, I need you to understand how serious this is. Someone not only broke into Dr. Porter's lab, but they also broke into our apartment. I'm not sure Webb did both of those jobs, but you need to be careful around him until we know who he is." Paul gives Sharina a stern look.

"You're not my dad, Paul. I'm as concerned as you are, so don't worry. I'll be careful. And you're killing the mood. Tell me how much you missed me." She kisses Paul again on his forehead and then softly on his mouth. The two embrace.

"I love you, Sharina." He kisses her lips again, with a little more passion. Then on her chest. "How's our little one doing?" he asks as he kisses lower, between her breasts.

Sharina loves that he's calling the baby *ours*. "You must be so tired and hungry…" she says as she kisses Paul again on his neck. Paul pulls Sharina's shirt aside and kisses her on her pinkish nipple. Sharina wriggles loose and closes the bedroom door.

***

"I am starved, and that smells so good," Paul says. "Let's clean up and go eat with the others? You use the bathroom first and I'll follow in a few minutes."

"Okay," Sharina replies. She looks at herself in the mirror above the dresser. She smooths her hair and walks to the bedroom door while Paul straightens out the bed. "Don't be long," Sharina says behind her. "I'll be out here interrogating our Mr. Webb."

Walking out of the bathroom, Sharina catches Chana talking to Mr. Webb in the dining room.

"I'm taking classes online, and finding lots of things around the three farms to occupy my time. What do you do with your time, Mr. Webb, when you're not breaking into people's offices and stealing files?" Chana is definitely on the offensive.

"Sorry, did I miss anything important?" Sharina walks into the dining room and sits down next to Teylen. "Where's Collin?" she asks. Teylen shakes her head, warning her not to go there.

"I was just answering Mr. Webb's question as to what I do with my time since moving out here to the farms." Chana smiles at Sharina, who then gets up and walks over to where Mr. Webb sits. She puts out her hand.

"I'm sorry," Sharina says to Mr. Webb. "I don't believe we've met. Sharina Mathews."

Mr. Webb looks at Sharina's hand. He takes his napkin off his lap, puts it on the table, and halfway stands. "Sean Webb, nice to meet you." He puts his hand in Sharina's, and Sharina gently reaches for Chana's hand on her other side. Everything freezes, even Mora. Everyone is still except Chana, Sharina, and Aaron, who sees Collin out in the front yard, moving about the fire pit.

"What are you doing, Sharina?" Chana asks from behind her.

"I'm getting to know our visitor. One second." Sharina continues holding both Chana's and Mr. Webb's hands for a few more seconds. Then she lets go. No one really notices that anything has happened except Chana and Aaron, who had stayed in Sharina's time. Sharina finishes shaking Mr. Webb's hand, then sits down. Aaron looks about to see if the time lapse registers on anyone's face.

"You're okay, Mr. Webb. Everyone here is friendly. Glad to meet you. Ma, would you pass me some of that chicken and the potatoes?" Sharina smiles at Teylen. "So, where is Mr. Webb going to be sleeping tonight? I think since we only have two people at Mom's house, maybe he should take the empty room there. What do you think, Mom?"

Teylen looks at Mr. Webb. "Yes, that would be fine," she says. "Or he could stay in the trailer next to the barn if he wants a little more privacy."

"I don't want to put anyone out," Mr. Webb says. "Either place is fine. Thank you for having me here."

Paul walks into the dining area and sits down next to Sean Webb. "You meet everyone?" Paul asks, leaning into Mr. Webb, who nods his head while biting into a piece of chicken. Aaron hands the potatoes and chicken to Paul, who loads up his plate. "Wow, this looks delicious! I have to say, I missed the good food while I was away."

"How were things in the West, Paul? I want to hear about your trip," Huang says as he finishes his dinner and leans back in his chair. "Go ahead and eat. You can catch us up later." Huang smiles, and Paul nods appreciatively.

"We'll go over to my mom's house and turn the heater on in the trailer when you're finished, Mr. Webb," Sharina says. "The pipes are all insulated, and it hasn't been cold enough yet for anything to freeze. You'll have some privacy there." Turning to Teylen, she says, "This chicken is delicious, Ma! Is it yours?"

"Yes, dinner was a joint effort," Teylen says, while getting up and cleaning off some dishes.

"Here, let me help you with that," Aaron tells her.

The room falls strangely quiet. There is small conversation about odd jobs around the farms that need finishing before the snow sets in. Sharina continues eating, never taking her eyes off Mr. Webb, who looks around at everyone while he eats.

From the kitchen, Aaron catches another glimpse of Collin, who is sitting in a chair outside by the fire ring, with Mr. Biscuit on his lap. Aaron points out the window and says to Teylen, "I'm going to head out and see if Collin is okay. I'll be right back to help you with those dishes. That dinner was excellent—thank you so much, Teylen. Don't do those dishes!"

Teylen nods.

Aaron grabs his coat off the hook, slips his boots on, and heads out to the side yard, where Collin has started a fire in the fire pit. The sparks leap and the wood makes a popping sound. "Hey, Collin," Aaron says, sitting down in the chair across from him. "What's up? Why did you leave?"

Collin looks at Aaron but remains silent for a moment. Finally he says, haltingly, "I'm just angry. I miss my cat and wish I knew who killed him."

"So you could do what?" Aaron asks.

Collin looks at Aaron. "You're right. I just never got to say goodbye. He was really the only family I had."

"Well, now you have more family than you know what to do with," Aaron points out. Then he changes the subject. "Hey, did you feel the freeze when Sha shook Mr. Webb's hand?"

"No, when did that happen?" Collin asks.

"Just about ten minutes ago. I saw you putting more wood on the fire out here while everyone else was frozen."

"Wait, what?" Collin asks, confused. "I've never not been affected before."

"I know," Aaron smiles. "Kind of cool, right? I wonder what's changed?"

"Maybe it's because I was outside? We haven't tested the theory we had that it is only frozen where Sharina is, and only for a brief time."

Aaron sits back and ponders. He would have to run this by Sharina and Chana, and see if they can explain what happened to Collin.

Mr. Biscuit jumps down from Collin's lap.

"Well, I guess I'm on dishes tonight," Collin says, and he slowly gets up to head inside.

"Me, too," Aaron says as he follows Collin. They make their way to the side door. Opening the door to the mudroom, they hear lively conversation coming from the dining room.

"You're not supposed to be doing those," Collin says to Teylen, who is bent over the sink full of dirty dishes. "You cooked, so scram."

Aaron grabs an apron off its hook on the wall and hands one to Collin, who slips it over his head and ties it around his waist. "Let's start with the silverware," Aaron says to Collin as he begins to gather it all up. Collin prepares a soapy bowl to soak it in. As the two move about the kitchen, Sharina's voice can be heard from the dining room.

"We do yoga in the morning, Mr. Webb," Sharina says to their guest. "It's at seven a.m., and we're hoping you can join us in Mom's barn. You can wear a pair of Paul's sweats, and I have an extra mat upstairs."

Aaron and Collin look at each other and laugh, both having experienced Sharina's morning yoga. "That ought to be interesting," Collin says out loud.

"I've never done yoga before," Mr. Webb's reply can be heard among the clanking dishes. "Sounds like fun! Count me in."

In the dining room, Minki is standing at Mr. Webb's side.

"All done?" she asks.

"Yes, thank you. That was delicious." Mr. Webb smiles up at Minki.

Not bad looking, Minki thinks to herself as she walks his plate out to the kitchen. When she turns around, she almost bumps into Mr. Webb with his hands full of dishes.

"I guess I need to be useful if I'm going to be here," Webb says. "I'll help in the kitchen with the dishes." As he sets the dishes down on the counter, he looks at Collin, elbow high in bubble water. "I'm sorry. I don't think I caught your name."

Collin side-glances Mr. Webb. "I'm Collin. Sorry if I was rude. Here," he says, handing Mr. Webb an apron. "You don't have many clothes; you'd better protect the ones you do have."

Mr. Webb stands next to Collin and puts dishes in the dishwasher as Collin hands them to him. Aaron busies himself with putting food into containers and into the refrigerator.

"I'm sorry about your cat," Mr. Webb says to Collin. "I promise you that isn't our style, and I didn't have anything to do with that. I could never do something like that. I'm a total animal lover."

"I'm sure," Collin says, handing Mr. Webb another dish. "I just miss him."

Minki walks into the kitchen and reaches for the radio knob. Music starts playing, and she begins humming as she moves around her kitchen, helping Aaron put things away in the refrigerator.

Conversation continues from the dining room. *Mr. Webb is fully assimilated*, Minki thinks to herself, watching him put the dishes into the dishwasher.

H AVING RETURNED TO TEYLEN'S FARM, Sharina and Mr. Webb make their way across the lightly snow-covered lawn and out to the trailer that is hooked up behind the barn. Paul watches from a window inside, unsure of whether, and to what extent, he should trust Mr. Webb, especially when he's alone with Sharina.

"Here, let me take that from you," Mr. Webb offers as Sharina carries a pile of towels and donated clothing for his stay.

Sharina hands him the stack. "Well, this is it," she tells him, as she reaches for the trailer door and opens it. She puts her hand inside and flicks on a switch. The trailer lights up, and Mr. Webb can see its curved wooden panels along the front, a small kitchen along one side, storage along the other side. "The bathroom is on the right, and the bedroom is all the way at the back," Sharina says, then moves out of his way so he can step up into the trailer.

Mr. Webb sets the stack of clothes down on the table and looks back at Sharina, standing at the open door.

"If you flick that switch up there and then turn the dial, you have heat." Sharina points to a set of switches and a dial plate between the kitchen and the bathroom. "And you'll only get hot water for about five minutes, so quick showers are a good skill."

Webb looks back at the small Abenaki woman, standing at the bottom of the trailer stairs. "So, Sharina, tell me, is it true?" Mr. Webb has brown eyes and dark hair. The hard dimple in his cheek makes him interesting when he smiles.

Sharina looks up at his face. "Is what true, Mr. Webb?" she counters, placing her long, black hair behind her ear.

"Have you and Chana conceived parthenogenically?" Mr. Webb sits on the top step of the trailer, bringing his face more in line with the young woman's.

"So the researchers say," Sharina smiles. "But I don't know why people think it's any more of a miracle than conceiving with another person."

"I suspect it's because not many women have been able to do that through history. I can only think of one," Mr. Webb says, chuckling lightly.

"And no one believed that woman then," Sharina says quickly. "Just think, Mr. Webb, maybe there are lots of women who've had the ability, but we just didn't know about them. It really isn't anyone's business but hers, is it, Mr. Webb?

Mr. Webb's mouth hangs open slightly.

Sharina continues, "And when I step back and look at humanity busting the seams of the planet with seven billion of us, who is to say Nature hasn't been devising another way for us to reproduce that automatically limits our numbers? Or perhaps She perceives the danger that centuries of patriarchy and capitalism and competition have brought upon the planet, and She wants to ensure that humans continue? I don't know why it's happening, but I do know that the baby is in my body, and therefore is really only my business."

"But you can't believe that!?" Mr. Webb sputters. "Surely you recognize the miracle of an asexual being? Of course the world is going to want to know about it, and I don't think you or I could stop that from happening."

"Maybe we can't. But maybe this has been happening for a longer time than people know? Women's matters don't seem to interest science nor the medical community until it's about a baby, and even more so if it's a boy. That makes it an easy thing to hide. I'm just asking that you stay with us here for a while, Mr. Webb, and give yourself a chance to get to know everyone. Think of it as a vacation?" Sharina steps back from the door and lets it go. It hangs open. Mr. Webb leans forward and reaches for the handle. As Sharina walks toward the house, she calls back, "Goodnight, Sean Webb. Remember, yoga, seven a.m. in the barn. Don't be late!"

Mr. Webb pulls the trailer door shut and surveys his new surroundings. There is a picture of Teylen and Sharina when they were both much younger. She is a child of about three, and Teylen is holding a chicken up for her to pet. The photo is black and white, printed on photo paper. There is also a map of Vermont tacked to the wall, alongside one of the U.S. On the map of Vermont someone has written "You Are Here" in red ink, pointing to just outside the town of Barton.

Webb walks back to the bedroom and switches on a light. There is a small double bed with a large, folded comforter at the foot of it. The trailer is clean, for the most part, although it looks as though someone has left some smoking materials in a small tray next to the table in the kitchen. Webb turns on the heater and then opens the door to step outside.

Once outside, he sits in a chair that has been placed next to the trailer. He looks up at the night sky. It is vast and clear. He is able to make out the Milky Way and several star constellations.

"Wow!" he says out loud, surprised by the number of stars he can see. Somewhere in the darkness, he hears an owl hooting and another one repeating the call from the other end of the pasture. He allows his mind to wonder, for a moment, about all of Nature, and life suddenly feels much larger than it does in the city, and yet simpler.

He looks over at the house where Sharina has gone. Lights are still on and he can see people moving around inside. *Such a peaceful place,* he thinks to himself. *Seven billion people…was she right about that?* Being without his cell phone has made him realize how dependent on it he has become. It feels good not to reach for the gadget.

The night is beautiful, and it seems to Mr. Webb he has never really seen it before. Getting up from his chair, he opens the door to his trailer and goes inside. "Jesus, seven a.m.?" he says out loud as he closes the door.

S HARINA OPENS THE MUDROOM DOOR and steps inside. Hanging her coat on the hook, she hears Collin and Paul talking in the common living area. She sits down at the kitchen table and listens.

"I'm telling you, Paul," she hears Collin say, "the pregnancy has made both Chana and Sharina a type of signal disrupter. Sharina walked past my computer and affected its ability to communicate with itself. And only on the DOD work."

"But why?" Paul replies. "What would be the purpose?"

"Maybe there is no purpose. Maybe it's just a byproduct of the energy that caused the spontaneous pregnancy in the first place?" Collin was holding Mr. Biscuit again, and Sharina could hear the cat jump down off of Collin's lap and trot into the kitchen to see her.

"And while we're asking questions," Collin continues, "maybe we should ask the question, 'Why us?' Doesn't it seem like we've all been pulled together into this somehow, and it isn't accidental? And now this new guy—even he seems to be part of it."

"It's okay, Collin. I'm fine not having all the answers and watching how it plays out. And for me, it's quite exciting to see everyone becoming part of this discovery. Are you wanting to leave?"

"No, just the opposite. I want to know more. And Paul, tonight when Sharina held Webb's hand and froze the moment with Chana's hand, I was sitting outside by the fire. I had kicked my shoes off for a moment and put my feet on the ground, next to the warm rocks around the fire. Aaron said he saw me moving around during the freeze. Even Mora was frozen, but I wasn't. What was *that* about?"

Sharina hadn't known this. *What **was** that about?* she thinks to herself. She had held Mr. Webb's hand so briefly, just long enough to let her and Chana get a good look inside his soul. She hadn't seen Collin outside the window by the fire ring.

Sharina gets up with Mr. Biscuit and walks into the room where Collin and Paul are sitting and sits down on the floor, folding the cat into her lap. "Maybe it has something to do with your shoes being off, Collin?" Sharina offers. "Or maybe the energy just freezes the people it doesn't need in that instance. For some reason, it wanted you involved?"

The three of them look at each other.

"Maybe," Collin says. "I also wonder if having my bare feet on the ground had something to do with my awake-ness at that moment. You know. My feet were grounded in Earth. The ground has a negative electrical charge, and with my shoes off, it neutralized positively charged ions through the ground. Somehow that kept me awake?"

Scientists! Sharina thinks to herself. *Always dissecting…* "But what about all those people at the farmers' market? It was a mild, sunny day; surely someone was barefoot there?" Sharina asks as she strokes Mr. Biscuit's head.

"They mostly had their shoes on, Sha. But maybe your skin has to be in direct contact with the Earth…to stay awake. If so, I'd like to know what would happen if you and Chana touched while your feet were both grounded. Maybe that would make something else happen?"

Sharina and Paul look at each other for a moment, their eyes wide. They had frequently had conversations about balancing the pregnancy in a healthy manner with the interests of science and experimentation. Then Sharina says, "Maybe, Collin. We'll have to test that theory out. But I'm pooped and heading to bed. Are you staying here tonight?"

"No, I'm heading to Lisa's. I have some early morning work to finish up at her place. Guess I'll be heading off down the road." Collin gathers up his coat from the mudroom and starts to leave.

"Oh, Collin. I have a gift for you." Sharina walks over to her bedroom and returns with a small box. "Open it."

Collin takes the box and opens it. He lifts a tiny, sleeping kitten out of the cotton-lined box.

"It was born wild, and the mother has stopped nursing it. I just fed him before dinner," Sharina says. "He will need some TLC. Lisa has everything you'll need. I had to promise her you'd have him neutered as soon as he's old enough."

The kitten is small and tiger-striped grays and black, with a velvety pink nose. Its tiny *mew* brings tears to Collin's eyes.

"I…thank—" Collin draws the kitten in close to his chest.

"It's okay," Sharina says. "I knew you'd be a good daddy."

Collin gathers up the little kitten, places it inside his scarf like a makeshift hammock, and then inside his coat. Tears are streaming down his face. "Goodnight," he says to Sharina and Paul as he pushes himself through Teylen's side door and steps out into the cold of night.

Walking alone on the road to Lisa's farm, Collin peeks down inside his coat at the little face that looks up at him. "You are so cute," Collin says out loud as he walks, reaching inside to touch the little nose. He feels the warmth of the kitten's body against his chest and smiles. The tears are still coming. "Your predecessor was one amazing cat. You'll have a lot of growing and learning to do if you're planning to follow in his footsteps." The cat mews his tiny sound and looks up, as Collin makes his way toward Lisa's farm.

THE TRUCK HAS BEEN WARMING UP for twenty minutes when Paul and Huang finally emerge from Teylen's house. The shopping list is long, and they have decided to get an early start and return for breakfast. Sharina has turned a light on in the top of the barn as she warms it up for morning yoga. Light is also coming from Sean Webb's trailer. Chana, June, and G'ma Luani are up helping Minki prepare breakfast, and there is smoke coming from Teylen's woodstove chimney. Precisely at seven a.m., Mr. Webb appears at the barn, dressed in Paul's sweats and looking ready for yoga.

Sharina walks out the mudroom door, across the yard, and toward the barn door. "Good morning," she calls out to Mr. Webb.

Mr. Webb raises his hand in greeting.

Teylen follows behind and closes the door to her house. June, Mora, Minki, Aaron, and Lisa are also coming up the road, with Collin following behind them. Everyone is moving.

"Come on in," Sharina says to Webb, and she stands with the barn door open, waiting for the others.

There are stairs leading to the upper part of the barn. The barn is enclosed and insulated at the top, and when Mr. Webb opens the door into the yoga room, he is drowned in a memory of going home after long terms away at school. The barn was his favorite hideout place, to think or just languish an afternoon away. He had forgotten about that part of his youth, and the flood of memories was a surprise. The room is warmly lit, and the maple plank walls and ceiling add to its warmth. A large, curved window comes all the way down to the floor and faces toward the woods behind the barn. Sean Webb walks over to one of the yoga mats and picks it up. Teylen is just coming into the room.

"You can lay it anywhere," Sharina says to Mr. Webb. "We usually face toward the window so we can catch the sunrise."

Mr. Webb lays the mat down and sits on top of it, watching the others enter the room. June and Chana come in and lay their mats down next to Mr. Webb, and Teylen lays hers next to them. Mora and Aaron come in looking very sleepy-eyed and set mats down behind them. The room is heated to about sixty-seven degrees, neither freezing nor super warm.

Teylen turns around to Mora and Aaron. "What happened to you two?" she asks. "You guys look beat. Did you sleep okay?"

Mora sits down on her mat. "We were awake last night discussing some things. We're okay, Teylen. Thanks for asking." Mora leans forward and touches Teylen's arm. "How about you? How are you doing with all these people at your farm?"

"I love it! I haven't had so much fun in years. Don't you worry about me. Minki and Lisa are also thrilled with the help they are getting on their farms. We're all doing fine."

Collin walks in and places his mat next to Aaron's. "Good morning," he says.

Sharina places her mat facing the group. "Good morning," she says to a chorus of mumbles. "Let's stand at the back of our mat…"

BREAKFAST AT TEYLEN'S INCLUDES Sharina, Paul, Mr. Webb, and Teylen. Sharina carries a stack of sourdough pancakes on a plate and sets it on the table. She sits down next to Paul, who has just washed up after his trip into town. Outside, snow has begun to fall, and Teylen has a pot of water boiling lightly on her woodstove.

"Help yourself," Sharina says to Mr. Webb.

"Thank you," he replies. "I am kind of hungry after that workout this morning. Usually I'm running to my office with a coffee in hand this time of day. How nice to sit down and actually have breakfast." Mr. Webb takes three pancakes and passes the platter to Paul.

"How long are you able to stay with us?" Paul asks Mr. Webb, sitting next to him at the table. "Do you think your bosses are wondering what happened to you yet?"

"I have to file a report soon," Mr. Webb replies. "I'm hoping Teylen can find me some work to do, so I'm not just a guest. Oh, and Teylen, I laid some cash on the mantle in the living room to help pay for supplies. I don't want to be a burden."

"You're not a burden, Sean." It's the first time Sharina has called him by his first name only. It feels like a barrier between them has come down since yoga.

Teylen returns to the table with a plate of ham and eggs. Everyone has a glass of fruit smoothie on the table in front of their placemats. Sean cannot remember ever feeling so welcome in a place, outside of his childhood home. "Please, take some eggs," Teylen urges.

The platter of scrambled eggs gets passed around and everyone dishes some up. Music is coming from the kitchen, and the whole house is very warm. Mr. Biscuit is perched on the back of the living-room sofa, watching everyone with his cat eyes as he purrs.

WINTER IN VERMONT CAN FEEL LONG. It often isn't until April that Vermonters believe the sun will return and Earth will warm up again. They call it the "mud season," when all the snow melts and the soggy sod underneath hasn't quite yet pushed up new grass.

Sharina and Chana sit in Minki's living room, sorting seeds from previous years. Minki had dated her seeds and wanted all the packages with a date older than 2000 to be tossed out. After the culling, the seeds had been placed back in their holders inside the small, manila envelopes, waiting for planting. As winter passed, the two young mothers had found themselves altering several pieces of their clothing to make them fit.

Huang, June, and G'ma Luani had been busy all winter, connecting with other farms in the area and working toward establishing a local farmers' market/food cooperative, so residents would not have to drive all the way into Burlington or Montpelier for "a quality food shopping experience," as Huang liked to call it. "Just a small store with mainly local, organic produce, meats, eggs, and dairy products." And Huang had not let go of the idea.

"This is a perfect location for the food cooperative," Huang had said to June last January, as they stood on a piece of frozen earth that had come up for sale. It's just on the outskirts of town and it has an old house built on it that will suffice for the start-up.

"Huang, there is so much work to be done on the house alone, just to make it good for a public market," June had told him. "We'll also need to buy freezers and coolers and a cash register and…"

But Huang had already thought through all of that. He was determined to make the leap from research assistant to something that was Earth-based and helped their neighbors as well as themselves. "We'll cash in my inheritance and build the store with that," he had said to June.

By the end of May, the fledgling co-op was up and running. The small house was painted bright yellow with a lavender door and planter boxes out front for flowers. They carried locally sourced foods, but they had also registered the store as an official food co-operative and were able to bring in other products the community loved having at their fingertips, such as organic potato chips and taco seasoning.

Opening day is hectic. Chana and Sharina are both working in the kitchen part of the store. Huang and June hired and trained people from the community to run the cash registers and receive and stock goods, which left them free to take inventory and place orders, as well as keep their eyes on the store.

The store sputtered and grew and gradually took shape with the help of the community.

In the co-op's kitchen, Sharina and Chana make sandwiches for the small deli section of the store. They both have to stay away from the computer equipment, since some type of magnetic or electrical interference transmits from them to the computer whenever they walk by. This had posed all kinds of challenges for them until Huang had another toilet and sink installed off the back of the kitchen, so they could use that instead of passing through the store to the public restroom. It also helped keep them more out of sight.

"I'm so frustrated with having to give up so much," Chana says to Sharina over the hum of the cheese slicer. "I miss my friends and my school. I didn't ask for this baby, and I find myself resenting it." She stops and sits on the barstool next to the co-op's kitchen counter. She looks up at Sharina. "How do you stay so calm about this? Why aren't you mad like I am!?"

Sharina flips the cheese slicer's switch to *OFF*. "I'm so sorry, Chana. I understand. I *do* get mad sometimes, but then I play out all the other scenarios and I come back to thinking this is the way my life is going. Maybe the idea that I was supposed to control everything was really the problem. If we're parthenogenic, as Mom says, we have only one shot at having a child. And we don't know where this is leading or even what it's completely about. I guess I've just given myself up to the adventure. And there seems to be something more powerful at play here. Look at what we can do when we connect with each other. Maybe I'm being selfish…" Sharina pauses and looks down at her pregnant abdomen. "I'm so glad you're here, going through all this with me." Her eyes are suddenly full of tears, and one lets loose down her cheek and to her chin before she wipes it.

Chana stands up. "I'm sorry," she says, hugging Sharina. "I think I'm nervous about the baby coming. Mora says everything is good in terms of the baby's placement and our health, but we're so young and I'm thinking we should be in a hospital to give birth." Chana takes one of Sharina's hands and with her other hand, wipes a tear away before it falls from Sharina's chin.

"Too dangerous, Chana. You know that. They would take our babies and maybe us, too. Mr. Webb has told us to stay out of any place where we have to register, and I think he's right. Besides,

Teylen, Minki, and Lisa will be there for us. They won't let anything bad happen, and Mora has just completed her certification to serve as a midwife. I know Mom wouldn't allow anything to happen that would hurt us or the babies."

"You're right, Sha, and I love your mom and her friends. And I love you, too, but what will happen to our babies? Are they going to go through this when they hit a certain age and have to change their lives around for an unplanned pregnancy? A pregnancy they carry perhaps without ever having had sex?"

Sharina pulls Chana close to her. They both feel their hands warm suddenly, and when they pull back, the golden glow appears but is different this time…stronger. Their bodies are encased in this golden warmth, and they are standing still, inside of it. Images of war and bombs and guns and children being shot in schools pass between them, as if on a TV screen but holographically, in mid-air. Then the images shake and fall apart, seemingly from the vibrations.

While still holding onto Sharina, Chana whispers, "What is it?"

"I think it's a message for us," Sharina whispers back. "Don't let go yet."

As soon as the images of war and death vibrate apart and disperse, images of a different Earth appear. People are living communally, in small groups. There is a large garden and a golden, domed spaceship lying in the middle of the garden, with vines growing all around the ship. The people look like they are from long ago.

"Is that image from the present, or from a long time ago?" Chana asks.

Sharina shakes her head. "I don't know, Chana. I don't understand it, either."

Then the images stop. The women let go of each other's hands and look at one another.

"Was that a spaceship? Like an alien craft, a UFO?" Chana places her hands on her baby. "Are we having alien babies?"

"I don't know what we are seeing, Chana. We need to talk to Mom and see if she has any insights. Let's finish up here and head back to the farm. Are you okay?"

"I'm okay. I just want to understand what we're seeing when that happens."

The two women hug each other as best they can with the babies between them.

"I have this pervasive feeling, Chana, that everything is going to be okay. That we're okay and only need to be patient." Sharina steps away and takes a peek out into the store to see if their connection had affected anything. She sees people shopping and walking around. June is talking to one of the cashiers, and Huang is apparently upstairs in his office. A tune from the eighties is playing in the background, throughout the store.

June's head turns, and she looks at Sharina. She raises her eyebrows, and Sharina waves nonchalantly, as if nothing has happened. Then she steps back into the kitchen and takes Chana's hand. "What do you want to do?" she asks.

Chana's head drops. "Okay," she says, sounding defeated. "Let's finish slicing this cheese and wrap things up here and go talk to Teylen. Then she flips the switch on, and the hum of the cheese slicer starts up again.

ARON, MORA, AND COLLIN sit in a booth at the front of a
tiny restaurant in town. Collin has his kitten in a backpack with its head poking out. Now named "Rocket"
after his insanely quick darts across Lisa's living room floor, the
kitten and Collin have become inseparable.

"Can I please get a saucer with some cream in it for my friend
here?" Collin asks the server. "I'm happy to pay for it." The server
smiles and goes back to the kitchen.

"I'm just worried about the girls' safety," Mora says. "I've taken
all the online classes that I can take, and I've completed the mid-
wifery classes in Burlington." Mora had been making the drive
twice a week into the city for class. It was a two-hour drive one
way, so she would stay overnight at a motel for the next day's class.
Then the two-hour drive back to the farm near Barton.

Two young men wearing baseball caps walk into the restaurant
and go to the counter to order. The two eye Aaron, Mora, and
Collin sitting in the booth. Then the big one with red hair turns
around. "Hey, aren't you some of the freakozoids from the farm?"
he says loudly across the restaurant. "I hear you have some kind

of alien being living out there, waiting to give birth to more alien beings."

Other customers turn around and look at the man speaking loudly. Mora places her hand on Aaron's wrist. "No fighting," she says. "They're just kids. Ignore them."

The server comes with a small saucer of cream and sets it down on the floor. "No feeding the little one on the table," she tells Collin. "What can I get you?"

"Oh, Laura, you can't wait on them," the young man at the counter says to her. "They're from that farm up the highway. They'll kill you with their laser eyes." He is laughing at his own joke when the server turns around and asks him to leave.

Aaron stands up. "No, that's okay. Let him stay. We have to be going now anyway." Collin and Mora scoot their way out of the booth and stand. Collin lets Rocket lap up a little of the cream from the saucer on the floor and then he sets a few bills on the table for the server.

"Let him stay?" the man says to Aaron. "Like, what? You own this town and get to say who stays and who goes? What exactly do you guys have up there at that farm?" The young man stays seated at the bar, turning just partway toward the booth. Like typical New Englanders, the other diners have gone back to their own business and ignore the loud youth.

Collin picks up his backpack and slips Rocket back into it. He heads to the door. Mora follows him. Aaron sets a couple more bills down on the table. "Thank you," he says to the server.

She mouths quietly to him, "I'm sorry."

Outside, the three get into the farm truck and start it up. "That's what the townspeople think," Collin says, "that we are all some kind of freaks living 'up at that farm.'" He looks at Mora seriously, and then they both start laughing.

As Aaron steers the truck toward the farm road and shifts into third gear, he says, "Maybe Teylen and the other farms should get some big dogs?" He looks in his rearview mirror and realizes the young men from the coffee shop are following them.

"We've got company, guys," Aaron nods toward the rearview mirror. Halfway down the farm road ahead of them, they see Chana and Sharina walking home from the food cooperative. Aaron has to speed up to pull over next to them before the other vehicle beats them there.

The car following them pulls up next to the driver's side of the truck. "Are those the women aliens?" the passenger asks, leaning forward to get a better look.

Sharina and Chana look across the bed of the truck at the young man and his friend in the car. Sharina grabs Chana's hand, and the car and its occupants freeze.

"Get in," Aaron says, and the two women get into the back seat of the cab, still holding hands.

Collin jumps out and punctures one of the tires on the men's car. Then he lifts the hood and removes a few things. "There," he says loudly to the frozen occupants of the vehicle. "Your car is all fixed—no charge!" He gets back into the truck, which then continues down the road, a glowing gold color coming from the backseat.

C HORES AROUND THE FARMS had increased with the onset of the planting season. Lisa's mushroom farm needed new wood logs for plugging. Collin had loaded the back of the truck with large pieces of maple and oak, and brought them to the south gate of Lisa's garden area, where he is unloading them.

Lisa stands at the gate. "Thank you so much, Collin. That's going to be great!"

"No problem, Lisa. I'll find time to drill the holes for plugs this weekend." Collin continues unloading the logs. Lisa had become a friend to him, a good friend. She had helped Collin nurse the small kitten back to health and into Rocket, a large, thriving male cat. Collin had taken Rocket to the vet, as promised, and had him neutered.

Lisa allows the cat to rule the roost, and Collin enjoys helping whenever and wherever he can. There would be a medium-sized harvest of mushrooms in the spring and then through the summer, with the biggest harvest happening in the fall. Most of the mushrooms took only a few months to reach full growth after the casings were put down. Collin found himself enjoying the farm so thoroughly that he had taken over much of the work. Lisa was able to do more marketing for her mushrooms, to restaurants and food co-ops around the state and in New York. She was building a reputation for herself, and many restaurants had her mushrooms on backorder, willing to wait for such a fresh, organic product.

"When the truck is empty, let me know?" Lisa says. "I'm going to take another batch in to a few restaurants in Burlington and do some shopping."

Collin waves. "Will do!" he calls after Lisa as she heads into the house. All three of the farm women have a similar walk, but Lisa walks with a bit of a limp from throwing her left hip out every time she steps forward on that foot. "It's just the way I came," she had explained to Collin when he asked about her limp.

Collin can see G'ma Luani next door, working in the chicken yard. She is out every morning, tending to those chickens like they had become her reason for being. Collin realizes that, for the first time in his life, he likes everyone he is around, all day long.

He thinks back to his family of origin and how his dad had held the family under his thumb with his violent temper and outbursts. Once he had turned thirteen, Collin had begun dreading being home and started looking for a way out. Graduating early and moving to California had been good for him. But then some of his fellow college students seemed to still have a high school mentality—someone always having to bully someone else—and being younger than most made him an easy target.

Collin had pretty much kept to himself in college and finished early. Professor Paul Stone had been one of the highlights of his college days. But never had he felt so at home and so at peace as he did now, living here. *I don't get it,* he thinks to himself. *I never would have pegged me for a farm person, yet here I am.*

TEYLEN IS SITTING AT THE KITCHEN TABLE with a snail-mail letter in hand when Sharina and Chana walk in, laughing. They both stop as soon as they see Teylen's face.

"What is it?" Sharina asks. "What is it, Mom?"

Teylen drops the letter down by her side and smiles. "How was town today?" she asks.

"Why are you changing the subject?" Sharina replies. "What does the letter say? Who is it from?"

Chana walks around to the other side of the table and sits down. Sharina remains standing near her mother and puts her hand on her mother's shoulder. "What is it, Mom?"

"It's a letter from Sean Webb. He says a search warrant was issued for Dr. Porter's office, and the people he works with went through her office. They said it was a matter of national security." Teylen looks at the young faces around her. "Don't worry. He warned Dr. Porter in advance, and she got important files out before going underground herself."

Sharina remembers back to the time when Dr. Porter was standing outside the campus rec center where she'd taught yoga, waiting to give her card to her so she could call Porter when things got rough. *She was warning me,* Sharina thinks to herself, *and now she is in hiding, with her lab being scrutinized.*

Suddenly a wave comes over Sharina and she can feel the past eight months catching up with her. She starts to shake, and barely manages to grab the table before falling.

Teylen pops up. "Here, Love, sit down."

Chana gets up and goes over to Sharina and sits close to her.

"What happens if they come here?" Sharina says to Teylen.

"Well, then they will get what they have coming to them, daughter of mine. Now don't you worry. Worrying is wasting life, and we are not going to do that."

Teylen walks over to the radio and turns it on. Chana and Sharina sit with their knees together, holding hands. When Teylen turns around, she sees they are both floating lightly above their chairs, wrapped in their golden orb. Teylen walks into it and places her hand on top of theirs. The images start appearing above them immediately: a long line of black vehicles coming down the farm road, and then everyone is holding a gun, and then their guns turn into flowers. Then the golden spaceship sitting in the garden, with plants growing all around it. Teylen lets go and Chana removes her hands.

"Wow!" Teylen says. "I've never had it that strong before."

"Had what?" Chana asks.

"The insight that just came in pictures. I've had super-brief insights, but nothing like that."

"That happened today at the Lavender House Co-op, when we were in the kitchen," Chana says.

Sharina looks up at her Mom. "What do you think it means, Ma?"

"I think it means you and Chana and those two babies are very powerful, and you don't need to worry. My tribe people used to call that a vision. You had a vision about the future. The thing about visions is, you have to be careful how you interpret them. They don't always appear the way things actually play out in the future. They are more of a hint or clue, and when the time comes, they will help you make the right decision. They are like guides."

Chana looks at Sharina. "We're being guided, Sha. We don't need to worry. You were right." Chana is uneasy seeing Sharina upset. She is her rock, and Chana needs her to stay that way. "They help us!" Chana bends her head down so Sharina has to look at her, and Sharina smiles. "We've got spiritual guides. We've got *spiritual guides!*" Chana says in a singsong way.

Sharina laughs slightly.

"Oh, there it is," Chana says. "There's that smile we all know and love." She gets up and walks toward the bathroom, singing a song that her mother used to play when she was little. "I am the eye in the sky, looking at you, I can read your mind. I am the maker of rules, dealing with fools..." and she closes the bathroom door.

Sharina grudgingly laughs. "What a nut!" she says loudly enough so Chana can hear her through the door.

"Yeah, but you love me," Chana shouts back.

Teylen smiles. "I sure like that girl!" she says, putting the letter in her apron pocket. Then she walks off, joining in, "...I am the eye in the sky, looking at you..."

MORA, TEYLEN, MINKI, LISA, JUNE, and G'ma Luani are all gathered in the yoga room early Saturday morning to give Sharina and Chana some prepping before the babies' births. Mora has brought pictures of babies in utero with their heads pointing down as they emerge from the womb. She also wants everyone to support Sharina and Chana in their breathing exercises, preparing them for a home birth.

"So," Mora says to Sharina and Chana, "the important thing to remember is that birth is completely natural, and billions of women have given birth before you—and lived. You will, too."

The women sit on cushions in a circle, and Mora has them all doing breathing exercises, learning to breathe through a contraction and taking quick, short breaths, to avoid pushing at the wrong time.

"What happens if I pass out?" Chana asks.

"You won't," Mora replies. "And if you do, I'll bring you back with some smelling salts. You both need to remember that this is completely natural. You're not sick. Nothing is wrong with you. You just need to allow the babies to come through you. It is a practice for letting our children go later in life, when they grow up. You have to let them go, and the birth will be fine. Just keep breathing."

"Some of those billions of women have died, though," Chana chimes in. "And lots of them are in hospitals when they give birth," she says to no one in particular.

Sharina takes Chana's hand. "We're not going to die, and we're fine here on the farm. Everyone will be here looking out for us. It's going to be fine, Chana."

"I know. I just feel scared, like something will be asked of me that I won't be able to do."

"You can do this, Chana. I know you can do this. You're strong and brave and you've got this," Sharina reassures her, and the others all nod.

"You're strong and brave, Sharina. I'm scared and a coward."

Sharina laughs a little. "I'm only brave because I have you, Chana. You're my strength, and I will never leave you through this. Let's trust in each other. We can do this. It will be okay. Right, Mora?" she says, turning toward Mora.

Mora had been watching birthing videos for six months now while she was taking classes in the city. She had found her vocation, and a renewed sense of joy and purpose had returned to her and Aaron's life. Their most solemn wish was for a baby of their own one day.

"It's going to be wonderful, Chana," Mora says as she moves on through the breathing exercises. "You'll see. When that beautiful baby comes out, you'll forget all of this worry."

Teylen gets up at the end of the lesson and asks that everyone push the cushions back and form a circle. The women clasp hands, and she has them all take three steps forward clockwise and one step backward, counterclockwise. "This is a dance my mother used to do with me to remind me that in life, there are setbacks…one step back. But then there are times when we really move forward…three steps forward. But of course, in the end, we are only in a circle and begin again."

The women stop and come in close to hug each other. Sharina and Chana are at the center of the circle, and the women all close in around them and do a big group hug.

Outside, Paul is just returning from a trip to California, to appease Kyle Christensen. He's relieved to be near Sharina and the farm again. As he comes up the road, the entire top part of Teylen's barn is glowing gold through the window. He parks his vehicle and races up the stairs to the top of the barn, thinking something bad has happened and Sharina and Chana are having to protect everyone. He opens the door to the yoga studio and is hit with golden light coming from the center of the room. All the women are floating slightly off the floor, and their heads are all bowed to the center with their arms around each other. Slowly, Paul steps back out the door and closes it. *Home sweet home*, he thinks to himself, smiling.

T HE RACE WASN'T AGAINST TIME; it was against evolution. The DOD had long known that evolution was creating a species of humans that could reproduce without sex. As far as they knew, this new chapter in humanity was female, creating only female children and only one child per mother. Despite the obvious implications for males, that wasn't what worried the DOD. Rather, its concern was the way these new female beings affected its technologies and machines. The electrical forces emanating from these females would gradually erode the signal of any technology that was created for destructive means, even if those means were not the intention of the technology. Guns would become inert. Atomic bombs wouldn't work. Artificial intelligence would all be redirected. It was a race in which Nature insisted on playing her card. As climate change worsened, the elimination of technologies would become more severe. Planes wouldn't fly. Internal combustion engines wouldn't work.

The estimated number of these new beings was only two thousand on all of the planet. But those were the known numbers. And to date, the DOD hadn't been able to locate and take into custody a single one of them without serious repercussions. So it was a race between those forces that profited off the destruction of the planet and this new evolutionary force that brought forth *humans who did Mother Nature's bidding. And the worst part was that when anyone from the DOD was able to infiltrate and get close to these beings, he or she would be neutralized through brainwashing to love Nature and healing and Earth, instead of working for the DOD. It was a huge threat.*

W HEN SEAN WEBB STEPS BACK into his office at the Pentagon six weeks after he had initially left for Vermont, he is whole. He had found what his life was missing, something essential that he didn't realize had disappeared. Sean had found a love for Earth and Nature, and for himself. Thinking back to who he was before landing at Teylen's farm, he doesn't recognize that person. So lost and clueless.

It had been Sean's decision to go back and cover his tracks. He needed to convince his superiors at the DOD that he had made an impromptu trip to visit his mother in New York.

"The plane ticket says you went into Burlington, Vermont," his boss had probed.

"My brother was there in Vermont, and he drove me into New York to see our mother. I apologize for the suddenness of it. She just had a bad moment and I needed to check on her."

And he hadn't been lying. He *had* gone to New York to visit his mother, who lived in a small brownstone, and his visit had been eventful. When he arrived at her door, he had stood outside for a moment. Then she had opened the door.

"Hi, Mom." Sean had never seen his mother so clearly. The guilt that had kept him away from her was gone. Now he just wanted to love her.

"Seany!" she had said, opening the screen door to get a closer look.

Sean had stepped into her foyer, and his mom had wrapped her arms around him and hugged him. In turn, he had enfolded her in his arms. *She has shrunken and is smaller*, Sean had thought.

"It's been too long, Mother," he said, fighting tears. "I'm so sorry."

"Hush," she said. "I don't want to waste one moment of you being here on apologies."

But Sean *had* owed her an apology. He hadn't visited her in more than three years, and his phoning had been relegated to just the holidays.

"I love you, Mom," he had said. It was something he hadn't been able to say in a long time. His resentment toward his father for leaving with a younger woman when he was in college had morphed into blame toward his mother, for some weird reason. She had always been patient and understanding and…there.

His mom had stepped back from him and looked in his eyes. "What's happened?" she said.

Her perceptions were keen, and Sean knew she sensed the change he had gone through on Teylen's farm. So he sat back and told her everything. About breaking into the doctor's research lab. About the farm and Teylen and living in the small trailer, under all the stars. About yoga and Paul and Collin, and the type of work he had performed while on the farm. But mostly, he had told her about the night Sharina had saved his life.

"I was in a bad place, Mom," he said. "Living on the farm and having people care about me and care for me made me realize how devoid my life was of people who cared. I need more people in my life, Mom. I was so down that night and hopeless."

It was true. Sean had been thinking about a way out for days. He knew he had to go back to his job eventually, but life on the farm had made him realize that returning was impossible. Then he had started to think of ways of ending it. He had sat under the stars that night, and while he was devising a plan, Sharina had come out of the house and walked over to him.

"I need you, Sean Webb," she had said, point blank, no explanation. "I need you to return to your job and let us know what is happening on that end. In return, I'll make you a promise. This trailer will always be your trailer. There will always be a place for you here. You are part of us, and this will always be your home."

Sean had literally broken down and bawled like a baby. Sharina kept an arm around his shoulders as he cried. She knelt next to him and kept telling him it was okay.

Two days later, a wooden panel had appeared on the front of the trailer. Collin had made it at Sharina's request. It read, "Webb's home."

And it was right. He was home here, a home like he had never had since childhood. And he had been surprised to come to understand just how much he needed home. *His* home. Where there was land and people and enough room to breathe clean air and talk and have a fire. A place where the stars shone so brightly at night you couldn't stop looking at them. A place where the women were happy and strong and the men were there to allow life to happen.

"I'll be back after this is over," he had told Sharina on the day he left to return to Washington, D. C., and report in to his bosses. "I'll be communicating and letting you know what I can. It will be through snail mail at the P.O. box. I'll miss you guys."

He had hugged Sharina. It was a long hug, and when he pulled away, she had said, "My turn," and hugged him back. "I'll miss you, Sean Webb," she had said. Then she had turned and walked back inside Teylen's house.

Sean had a friend he loved, something that had been so painfully missing from his life.

"You need to OK your time off before leaving, Detective Webb." Sean's commanding officer's unfriendly voice brings him back into the room. "Your perfect record and having never missed a day of work in twelve years motivates us to overlook your lack of warning about your need for time off. But from now on—"

"I know, Sir. I will be sure to put in for time off from now on when I visit her. I was just afraid I was going to lose her and didn't have time to put in the request and then wait for a response. I just had to go."

"And how *is* your mother, Mr. Webb?" His boss's eyes look up at him inquisitively.

"Oh, she's much better now, Sir. She needed me there and I needed to be there. We hadn't seen each other in a long time, and I think my visit did us both a lot of good. Thank you for asking, Sir."

As Sean leaves his boss's office, Commander Isley shoots a message off to his secretary. *Locate Inspector Webb's family background, please. Send it to me ASAP.*

THE GRASS IS VERY GREEN at the end of June, and the deciduous trees have leafed out in green fullness everywhere, slowly turning to the deeper shades of summer. Sharina and Chana walk barefoot along the riverbank, enjoying the summer day.

"Here," Sharina says to Chana. "This was my fishing spot when I was a kid." They bait their hooks, cast their lines into the river, and seat themselves in the coolness on some rocks alongside the water. Both women are on track to give birth within the next six days. Teylen had suggested that their births would probably synch up with each other, since their dates of conception were so close together.

"Wouldn't that be great if the babies came at the same time?" Chana says, holding her pole while watching how Sharina is holding hers, in an attempt to pick up some of the subtleties of fishing.

"That *would* be great," Sharina says, smiling. But there is something gnawing at the back of her mind. She doesn't quite know what it is yet, but she's aware of its presence. It's as if she and Chana have traded places and Sharina has become the worrier, while Chana seems more relaxed, resolved, stronger. Sharina tries to let it go and just keep enjoying the day with Chana. The young women had needed some relaxation time, away from everyone's worrying.

"So when the fish nibbles on your line," Sharina says, "you're going to give it a quick tug to make sure you've really hooked it. It's referred to as 'setting the hook.' Then you start reeling it in."

"How will we kill the fish so they don't suffer too much?" Chana asks, her brow furrowed.

"I'll do that," Sharina assures her, "until you have the hang of it. Then you have to do your own killing. Death is part of life, and taking a life is serious business. So we only take what we are prepared to eat. Nothing more. And we give thanks and respect to all beings that we consume."

"How do the masses of cows that people eat have respect?" Chana says while dipping her toe into the cool water. "Seems pretty disrespectful to keep them all under one roof, never knowing a green pasture and suffering most of their lives."

"Okay, Chana, we're not going to save the world here. It's just important that we understand it."

Chana smiles at Sharina's rebuffing.

"But yes," Sharina continues, "most mass production of meat is cruel to the animal, to humans, and to Earth. It's about numbers and profit and has lost sight of caring and heart and health. You're right. It's sad."

Suddenly Chana's fishing pole bows, and she quickly yanks it back.

"Good one!" Sharina says. "Now reel it in!"

A large trout makes waves across the water's surface as it struggles against the hook, and Chana attempts to reel it in.

"Oh, wow!" Sharina says. "That's a beauty! Keep reeling! You're doing great!" She wedges her pole into the rocks to free her hands. As Chana pulls the trout closer to shore, Sharina grabs for the net and scoops it up. Quickly she reaches into the net and pulls the fish out. She locates her surgical pliers and removes the hook from the fish's mouth. She reaches into its mouth and gives it a quick snap backward, killing the fish instantly. Holding the fish to her heart, she gives thanks and love to its being and to Nature.

"Nice one!" Sharina says. "That has to be at least a three-year-old. Look at that!" She pulls out her makeshift tape measure, which is her hand's span. "It has to be about thirteen to fourteen inches long. That's the biggest trout I've ever seen, Chana! Congratulations!"

Chana stands, beaming.

"Did you see how I quickly removed the hook and snapped the fish's neck?" Sharina asks.

"I'm not sure I could do that," Chana replies.

"Of course you can. I'll let you do it on the next fish, and I'll walk you through it." Sharina places the fish in the cooler while Chana rebaits her hook and throws it back into the stream.

"That was exciting!" Chana says. "I hope everyone likes river trout."

"Anyone who doesn't like river trout is a fool who doesn't deserve a good meal," Sharina says.

Wow, Chana thinks. *That's about the most unforgiving thing I've ever heard Sharina say about people.* "You feel strongly about fish," she ventures.

Sharina blushes a bit and bows her head. "Yes, I do. Streams and rivers are Earth's veins, and the fish are Earth's greatest gift to humans. Being able to walk out behind the farm and pull food from the river is truly a present of sorts. Anyone who fails to recognize the importance of that gift doesn't deserve it."

Suddenly Chana's line tugs again, and she yanks the pole and starts reeling.

"You've got another fish!" Sharina says, a little too surprised.

"Of course," Chana laughs as she's reeling the fish in. "You're a good teacher." As she continues to work the fish in close to shore, Sharina grabs the net and steps into the riverbank mud to scoop the fish up. It's another big trout.

"I've never seen anything like this," Sharina says as she nets the fish. "Okay, you get the surgical pliers to pull the hook out."

Chana carefully picks up the pliers and holds the fish in her other hand, the fish still wrapped in the net.

"Now just walk the hook back out the way it came in," Sharina says.

Chana carefully walks the hook out.

"That's it," Sharina says. "Now stick your thumb into the fish's mouth and snap the neck backward."

Chana reaches in, gives the fish's neck a quick snap, and the fish stops moving. Then she begins to cry. Hard.

"It's okay, Chana. You're okay." Sharina takes the fish from Chana's hand and puts it in the cooler. She brings Chana in close to her and holds her. But Chana can't stop crying. "Everything dies, Chana. We'll die, too, someday, and everyone we love will also die someday. I just see it as birthing into something else. Part of the natural cycle of living."

Chana opens the cooler and takes out her second fish. She holds it close to her chest and places her other hand over its head. "Thank you, and I'm sorry," she says, tears still streaming down her face. Then she replaces the fish in the cooler.

She's so city-raised, Sharina thinks to herself, *that she doesn't understand how much more humane this is than buying meat at the store.*

"I do *now*, though," Chana says, as if reading Sharina's thoughts. The two look at each other, realizing what has transpired. "You read my thoughts!" Sharina says, somewhat indignant but mostly surprised.

"It's as if the knowledge just becomes mine, very fast. As if you passed it to me when you had that thought."

"That's new, huh?" Sharina replies, raising her brows. She and Chana had become used to not questioning the unusual things that had been happening around them as they came more fully into their pregnancies.

Chana rebaits her hook and casts her line into the river.

"Boy, I'm having no bites today," Sharina says, "while you're having beginner's luck. It's not fair!"

Chana laughs.

"Hey, look at this." Chana pulls her legs in and puts the bottoms of her feet together. She levitates about a quarter inch off the rock. The two women laugh.

"How do you get the bottom of your feet together like that? I'm the yoga teacher and I can't do that." From inside the river's protective brush, the two women laugh and continue fishing.

T EYLEN HAD FELT THE CAR before she saw it coming down the narrow driveway. She had phoned both Minki and Lisa. Lisa had alerted Collin and Aaron, but Mora was in Burlington at one of her meetings and not due back for two hours. And Minki had phoned Huang, June, and G'ma Luani, who were in town at the Lavender Door Co-op.

Aaron reaches Teylen's house first, having had the same feeling that a car was coming. He bursts into Teylen's kitchen, somewhat out of breath, to find Teylen sitting on the kitchen floor's rug, cross-legged and meditating. She pauses to look up at him.

"Sharina and Chana are fishing and trying to relax," Teylen tells Aaron. "I'm sending to Sharina mentally so they stay there." Teylen closes her eyes and continues: *Just stay where you are and enjoy the day*. She runs the mantra over and over in her head while doing breathing exercises. "Paul's in the barn," Teylen quickly tells Aaron while continuing her chant.

When the car, a black SUV, pulls into Teylen's driveway, Teylen, Paul, and Aaron are ready for it. After the car stops, five men get out quickly.

Five *armed* men.

Paul and Aaron continue stacking wood in the barn and watching through the lower windows that are built into the large doors. From here they can view the entire driveway, and they see the men walking up to the side door of the house.

Teylen answers the door, and the men push their way into the house.

***

"Really, Paul," Teylen had insisted earlier. "It's the best way. I will disarm them. I'm a grown woman, and they have no interest in me. You are like dynamite. You're Sharina's man, and where you are, she probably is. Just stay quiet in the barn. Pretend to be stacking wood if you see them heading for the barn. Act like you didn't know they were coming. You don't know where your girlfriend is. 'Why do you want my girlfriend?' You know. Act like Sharina and you are pregnant together in the traditional way and these men are mistaken. Act incredulous if they come into the barn. Be indignant!"

Paul could hear the shaking in Teylen's voice and sense the adrenaline coursing through her body. *But she is right*, he thinks. *I would just bring more focus on Teylen and the farm.* Fortunately, he had the foresight to install a small microphone in the kitchen and another one in the living room, so he could hear what was going on from the barn.

***

"Look, Mrs.—" one of the men says to Teylen.

"Teylen, please. Call me Teylen—or Ms. Mathews, if you prefer."

The man is tall but average-looking and white, and had been born with a serious face, Teylen observes. *Must feel accomplished*, she thinks to herself. *I can give him that.* "It must take a lot of work to become an investigator for the United States of America," she says to the man. "I'd be so proud if I had a son like you. That's a real accomplishment. To what do you attribute your success?"

"Uh, thank you, Ma'am."

"*Teylen*, please."

"We're looking for your daughter, Sharina Mathews."

"Sharina? Whatever for? Is she okay? I just spoke with her last night. She's returning from France, you know? She's working with some of the biggest names in yoga to produce a book. Why are you looking for her?"

"Please, M'a—Teylen," the man fumbles. "We need to speak with your daughter immediately. Can you give us her number?"

"Won't you men please sit?" Teylen motions to her kitchen table and chairs. Everyone sits except the man who has been talking. "Can I get anyone a glass of water?"

"Ms. Mathews!" The standing man almost shouts. He pauses and collects himself. "Please, Ms. Mathews. Your daughter?"

Teylen stands erect and fearless in her kitchen before the suited man. "Well, frankly, Sir, you don't have any right to know where my daughter is, unless you explain what you want to see her for. I don't give her phone number out to just anyone, you know. She's a lovely young woman. So telling you where she is would make me a bad mother, and I don't want to be a bad mother…"

"Ms. Mathews." The man leans toward Teylen, who remains standing, still.

The kitchen is silent for a moment. Then Teylen speaks. "No, Sir. You come back with a warrant or something like that. Then I'll consider giving you information on where she is. I just can't help you, see? I don't know what it is you want her for, and she's my daughter. I love her with all my heart. I would never do anything to hurt her."

"I understand, Ms. Mathews, but this is of the utmost importance. We have the authorization to take you into custody if we need to."

"Well, you just go right ahead, Sir, if that's what you need to do. I'm not going to tell you where my daughter is unless you tell me why you need to talk to her. What could my Rina have to do with anything you're about? It's out of the question. I'm prepared to go." Teylen puts both her arms straight out as if waiting to be cuffed. She looks up at the tall, suited man from a good foot below him. "Go ahead, Sir," she says.

"Uh," the man shifts his weight from one foot to the other and looks at his suited colleagues. "That won't be necessary, Ma'am—er, Teylen. We'll return later with the requisite paperwork. We understand. You want to keep this professional, and we don't blame you. Come on, guys." As he beckons toward the other men, he starts backing out of the kitchen. "We didn't mean to be a bother. We'll talk to you later today or tomorrow morning when we have that paperwork."

The men all get up and head for the back door. At that moment, Teylen spots Chana and Sharina coming up the walk, just outside the door. She sees Aaron race out and quickly lead them into the barn.

"You guys came all the way out here for nothing," Teylen says. "Please, let me offer you a piece of cake?" She uncovers a beautiful cake with a few slices taken out of it. "We made it just yesterday and, lucky for you, no one ate here last night but my neighbor and myself." Teylen can see Sharina and Chana heading into the barn and the door shutting behind them.

"No, thank you, Ms. Mathews," the man says. "Maybe later, when we return with that paperwork?" He reaches for the doorknob and turns it. The five men walk out of the house.

"I NEED TO GO HELP MOM, PAUL!" Sharina glares at her husband, who insists that she stay in the barn.

Chana sits in the chair next to the barn door, terrified.

"Listen, Sha…" Paul pleads with her. "Teylen doesn't want them to see you. We have this worked out—"

Just then, Aaron sees the men open the side door to Teylen's house and start to pour out onto the stepping stones that lead to the driveway. He slowly raises his index finger to his mouth and mimes, "Shhhhhh." No one moves. Chana looks visibly ill.

The men's footsteps can be heard as they walk to their car on the graveled drive. The men open the car doors and get inside. The doors slam shut.

Aaron raises his finger to his mouth again, "Shhhhhh," and he lifts the index finger on the other hand toward Sharina as if to say, "Wait!" No one moves. Then Teylen's voice comes booming over a speaker on the wall near Paul's head as the men back out of the driveway.

"Good Goddess, have mercy!" Teylen cries. "Don't come out yet, Paul. Wait until you can't see their car. Keep Rina and Chana in there."

Paul motions toward Sharina. "See?" he says silently, pointing toward the speaker.

"Okay, you guys," they hear Teylen say. "They're out of sight."

PAUL, AARON, SHARINA, CHANA, and Teylen are in Teylen's kitchen when the others come over. Collin walks in with Minki and Lisa. Huang, June, and G'ma Luani are still in town at the food co-op, and Mora hasn't yet returned from Burlington.

"Why didn't I feel it, Ma?" Sharina moans. "I should've known they were coming. I should've been here to protect you."

"I'm the mother!" Teylen nearly shouts.

Everyone stops and looks at her.

"I'm supposed to protect you," Teylen continues, "and you are not the only one whose powers are gaining strength as your little one gets bigger. I sent you signals so you wouldn't come. Yes, I can do that now!"

No one says a word.

Then Paul turns to Sharina. "Sha, we were all okay. We didn't want to risk having you here and having them find you and Chana. We both felt it was best you didn't know they were here." His face is flushed from the excitement and worry.

Sharina sits down.

Chana takes advantage of the moment to ask, "What did they want? Why were they here, if they thought we weren't here?"

"They're looking for you guys," Teylen says, "and they probably aren't going to quit until they find you. This just bought us some time. They will return." Teylen looks at Sharina and then at the others.

"When?" Collin asks. "Do we know when they'll return?"

"Maybe as soon as tonight," Teylen replies.

Just then, Sharina and Chana move toward one another and hold hands. Golden color comes off their hands as everyone watches.

The back door opens and Mora walks in. "Hi guys, what's up?" she says. The sound of water splashing onto the floor follows, and Sharina and Chana look up at Mora.

"I think our waters just broke," Sharina says.

"And they broke at exactly the same time," Chana adds.

Mora quickly sets her bag down and comes over to the two young women, who continue holding hands while the others rush about, preparing for what could be two long labors. Sharina and Chana hover slightly off the floor, and their water on the floor lends the room a fragrance of flowers.

"We need to go out to the garden," Sharina tells Chana. And without letting go of each other, they move toward the garden area behind Teylen's farm.

Mora falls in behind them, looking concerned.

"Let them go," Teylen says. "It's a warm July afternoon, and the garden is a good place to give birth. We will take some blankets out. You go with them, and I'll bring water and our birth bag."

Paul stands next to Sharina as they walk out the door. He is trying to dial Huang, June, and G'ma Luani at the co-op. Finally, Huang picks up.

"It's time!" Paul says exuberantly.

"Hi, Paul!" Huang says loudly, and then whispers, "They're here now…" followed by his normal voice saying, "Okay, Paul. I'll keep those orders for you here as long as I can. I got to go."

"The women are in Burlington, just returned from France. That's the story, Huang. We'll take care of Chana. Be safe." Paul hangs up the phone and turns to the others as he helps Sharina and Chana out to the garden. "The Feds are at the co-op," he says, while helping the women move slowly. Chana looks at Paul. "It's okay, Chana. Your dad can handle the Feds. He is doing fine. He'd want you to focus on yourself right now."

Collin has run out ahead and spread a blanket and cushions in the center grass area of the garden. The two women settle down on the cushions, and Mora, after washing her hands, follows behind Teylen with a small medical bag. The chickens inside Teylen's chicken yard all stand at the fence, peering into the garden. Mr. Biscuit sidles up next to Sharina, who pets him.

"How are we doing?" Teylen asks Chana and Sharina.

"Well, if the rest of it is as easy as breaking water, I'm good," Chana smiles at Teylen.

Minki shows up in her truck, with Lisa in the passenger seat. The two women unload a standing privacy screen with Asian imagery on it. Walking out into the garden, they see the others. "We brought a privacy screen in case you guys decide to stay out here for the birth," Minki says. She walks over to Sharina and kisses her on her head, then goes to Chana and kisses her, too.

Lisa and Mora busy themselves with the medical supplies and equipment. Teylen walks back inside with a few of the instruments and sets them next to her stove. She gets out a large pot, fills it with water, and sets it on the stove to boil. Then she places the radio in the back window, where everyone can hear it from the garden, and turns it on. It's two o'clock, and Teylen knows it is going to be a while before any babies are born. She grabs up a couple of popsicles she had bought for this occasion and walks back out to the garden.

"Sit down, you two," Teylen says to Paul and Collin, who are pacing around the outside perimeter of the garden. She hands a popsicle to Sharina and another to Chana.

"Ah, thank you, Ma. Yes," Sharina calls to Paul, "you're making me nervous. Come sit down." She pats the mat next to her.

"You can rub my feet if you need something to do," Chana says to Collin, who promptly picks up her feet and begins rubbing them. "I feel like such a princess," Chana laughs.

***

By six o'clock, both women have started into serious labor. Collin helps Chana walk around the outside of the garden, and Paul walks with Sharina. Aaron stays out in the front, keeping an eye on the road.

Mora is sitting in a chair, eating a popsicle. Earlier she had sent the men away and measured both women's dilation; they were at five centimeters. "You're halfway there!" she had told them. What she found interesting was that both women were completely in synch. Despite having some uncomfortable contractions, they remained on their feet, walking the perimeter of the garden.

Sharina insists that everyone take off their shoes when near her and Chana. "I need your feet on the ground so no one freezes when Chana and I touch," she explains.

"Chana, your family is coming down the road," Aaron yells over the fence top toward the garden. "They're walking and will be here soon!"

At seven p.m., June comes walking up the road with G'ma Lu-ani, who goes inside to lie down. June opens the back gate to find her daughter walking around, with Collin supporting her. Chana is working through another contraction.

"Mom, you're here," Chana says, reaching for June.

"We had to walk from the highway. We hitched a ride secretly off a shopper who dropped us off at the top of our road. G'ma needed to go lie down." June stands on the other side of her daughter. When she touches her, the pain of the contraction seems to be significantly less.

"Wow, Mom. That contraction got easier with you here," Chana says.

Hearing this, Sharina thinks about it and makes a decision. "I think all the women need to embrace in a circle with us. You guys can stand on the outside, behind each one of us. Collin, you take Chana; and Paul, you're here," she points to the space behind her. Everyone looks a little confused. "I just suspect that our labor will go easier with us all connected," Sharina explains.

So Teylen, Minki, Lisa, June, and Mora make a circle that includes Chana and Sharina. They all walk slowly in the circle. "Here comes another one," Chana says. Both she and Sharina have trouble walking through the contraction. They bow their heads while the others hold them. Then it passes and the circle begins moving again, slowly. Chana looks up at Sharina. "I'm really scared," she says.

Sharina walks over to Chana and takes both her hands. Suddenly the backyard is glowing a gold color. Aaron's head pops back up, to be seen over the gate.

"The Feds are back. Everyone stay as quiet as possible! I'll try to keep them out here."

The black SUV pulls into the driveway, and the men get out. The garden is not visible from the driveway, but the radio playing may bring them outside. Everyone looks worried.

"You go," Teylen says to Paul. "Tell them Sharina won't be back until day after tomorrow. Try to get rid of them with Aaron."

Paul hugs Sharina. "Go, I'll be okay." Sharina smiles to reassure Paul, who leaves reluctantly. He quickly opens the garden gate and walks out onto the driveway, where the men, all wearing suits, are standing, hands on hips, looking around. There are only three of them, Paul notices. The other two must have stayed at the co-op with Huang. Aaron and Paul exchange glances. With a small tilt of his head, Paul motions for Aaron to take his place out back. Aaron walks around to the rear entrance of the garden area.

Paul raises a hand in greeting. "Hello. You guys must be the men Teylen told me about. You're from the government, is that it?" The men turn toward Paul. The evening is beginning to cool. "Welcome," Paul says, extending his hand. "Paul Stone. How can I help you?"

The tallest man shakes Paul's hand and hands him a search warrant. "You can tell us where your girlfriend is, Mr. Stone. We're pretty sure she's living here."

"Ah yes, well, Sharina is living here with her mother and me. But I'm afraid she's out of town in Burlington with a friend until the day after tomorrow. She just came back from a writing conference in France. I could have her call you when she gets back here, but you still haven't told us what this is about." Paul tries his best to smile.

Everyone's head turns at the sound of a vehicle coming down the gravel road. It's Huang's truck, with the two other men inside. He parks behind the large SUV. Huang gets out on the driver's side and walks over to Paul.

"Hey, Paul. I see you've met our visitors," Huang says.

The two other men join their coworkers on the driveway.

"Huang," Paul says. "So good to see you. Yes, I was just telling Mr.—"

"Hammond," the man offers.

"Yes, I was just telling Mr. Hammond that Sharina and your daughter are in Burlington until the day after tomorrow."

Mr. Hammond begins to look around the property. "You wouldn't mind if we walked around, then, would you, Mr. Stone?"

"No, feel free. Would you like to come inside and have something to eat? It is the dinner hour, and I'm famished."

Mr. Hammond agrees to go inside, but only for a look around. As Paul walks ahead of Mr. Hammond, he quickly takes a peek into the back garden area and sees that everyone is gone. Mr. Hammond goes inside alone while the four other men walk around the yard.

"I'd really like to know what it is you need to talk to Sharina and Chana about, Mr. Hammond. We're starting to feel a little harassed here." Paul looks sincerely into Mr. Hammond's face.

Hammond turns and walks to the back of the house, looking in every room. "I think you know why we're here, Mr. Stone. Both your wife and—"

"Girlfriend," Paul interrupts. "She's my girlfriend. We aren't married…yet."

Hammond's face hardens. "Both your girlfriend and her friend are of interest to us because they seem to be able to conceive naturally, on their own, we have heard. We've also heard that the pregnancies have created some type of data disrupter, and that makes it our business."

"Where did you hear all these crazy things?" Paul looks at Hammond like he's from another planet.

"I'm not at liberty to talk about that. Suffice it to say, we have our connections."

Paul's face is burning as he tries to walk back his anger. "Well, your connections have led you astray, Mr. Hammond. I assure you, there is nothing special about my girlfriend's pregnancy. We did it the old-fashioned way, if you catch my drift. And her friend just happens to be pregnant at the same time, so they are keeping each other company. No special powers, Mr. Hammond."

"Right." Having walked through the whole house, Mr. Hammond moves toward the back door. "I'm going to go talk to my co-workers outside, if you'll excuse me?"

"That's fine, Mr. Hammond. And if you'll excuse me, I'll be phoning our lawyer and getting his opinion on this." Paul pulls his cell phone out of his pocket and holds it in the air.

Hammond heads outside to reconnect with his accomplices.

"Damn!" Paul says out loud. He runs to the window where he can see Hammond and the others walking around the house, surveying the yard. Suddenly they all freeze. Paul realizes nothing and no one is moving—except him. He looks down at his bare feet; he's still moving. Quickly he reaches for the door handle and races toward the forested area across the river's footbridge, where everyone had agreed they would meet if the Feds arrived. He runs past the frozen federal agents in the backyard and toward the golden light that is shooting up from the meadow clearing.

"Sharina, I'm coming," he yells as he approaches the glowing, gold-hued air. He can see Sharina and Chana in the center of the women's circle. All the women have their hands on Sharina's and Chana's shoulders. The two young women are holding each other up while they push, their hands intertwined.

Suddenly the forest floor seems to drop about an inch, and there is a loud noise that comes from the center of the circle. Mora and Teylen move to the inside of the circle and place their hands on the babies' heads as they begin to emerge.

Paul races for the golden orb of light that emanates outward from Sharina and Chana. As the babies emerge, a loud cry can be heard throughout the forest. All the animals seem to pause and take notice of the light and the human cry.

Gradually Chana begins to drift upward, above Sharina's head, and the two women can't hold on to each other any longer. As their fingers slip from one another's, both babies emerge from their mothers' wombs, Chana's baby girl free-falling, followed by the afterbirth. Collin lunges forward and catches her, and Mora catches the placenta.

Chana continues rising upward, toward the heavens. Teylen is holding Sharina's baby in the soft blanket she has brought along. "Nooooooo!" Sharina screams as she frantically claws the air in an attempt to reach Chana, who continues moving upward. Chana's face looks peaceful, resigned.

A quick light cuts the overhead horizon, and Chana is gone.

June falls backwards into Huang's arms, turning her face into his chest.

Everyone stands in shock as the golden light begins to subside. It is quiet except for the sound of newborn humans crying in the forest, accompanied by June and Sharina's weeping. Teylen walks over to Sharina and places her baby girl in her arms.

"Don't cry, child," Teylen says softly. "It is the way. Look, she is beautiful."

Collin walks over to where Sharina lies in the tall grass. He places the other infant in her arms. Sharina looks up at Collin's face, searching for some kind of explanation.

"She's gone, Sharina," Paul says quietly from behind her. "We're not supposed to understand it. She's just gone." There is a long pause. "I love you, Sha. You did it. Don't cry." Sitting behind her, he creates a backrest with his chest for Sharina to lean into while holding the babies. "They're beautiful," he says. And the babies *are* beautiful—pink and full of life.

Sharina sees June crying into Huang's chest, and she hands Chana's baby to Paul and motions toward June. Paul stands up with Chana's infant, and walks over to her. He places the baby in June's arms. "Your grandchild," he says softly. June looks up and sees the infant. Carefully Paul releases her and backs away.

"Look, she's beautiful," June says to Huang. Her tears fall softly on the baby's face.

Teylen, Minki, and Lisa begin singing a song that Sharina knows well. It is one she grew up with, about the mighty power of those who live in the stars, and the love they bestow upon those who live on Earth.

June looks down at Chana's baby lying in her arms, and her tears continue to drop onto the blanket the baby is wrapped in.

"Oh, she is lovely," June says, turning her body toward Huang so he can see the newborn. The new grandparents smile. Huang wraps his arms around June and the newborn, but he cannot stop looking up toward the sky, the place where he last saw his daughter.

The sky begins to darken as evening falls upon the small farm. Everyone stays in the forest clearing while Paul digs a deep hole just outside their circle. Teylen places both afterbirths into the hole, and Paul buries them.

"Mark that somehow," Teylen says, "and we'll plant a tree there."

The ground begins to glow a golden color where they have buried the afterbirths. "Something tells me I won't need to mark it," Paul says, looking at Teylen. Everyone is gathering up their things to move back into the house.

"Let Collin and me check to see what's going on with our visitors," Paul says as he reaches for Collin's shoulder. The two men make their way through the forest toward the backyard garden. As they come to the house, Paul sees the men sitting in their car, on the driveway.

"Wait," Collin says, grabbing Paul's arm as he begins to move toward the car. "What are you going to do?"

"I'm thinking it will be like the farmers' market and I won't have to do anything. Stay close." Paul and Collin walk hesitantly toward the men's car. Paul taps on Hammond's rolled-up window. Slowly Agent Hammond's window comes down and he looks out at Paul.

"Good evening, gentlemen," Paul says in through their window. "Is there something I can help you with?"

The men inside the car appear dazed. The driver looks out his window at Paul. "Where are we?" he asks. "How did we get here?"

"You had just stopped here and asked for directions because your phone wasn't working. You must've made a wrong turn somewhere back at the highway. If you just head up this road, you'll find the highway."

Agent Hammond, the driver, unconsciously nods and puts up his window. The engine turns over, and slowly the SUV heads toward the highway.

"And good riddance," Collin says slowly in a calm voice, over Paul's shoulder as the SUV begins to disappear up the road.

***

It is night, and the stars are shining brightly. Silence has fallen around the farms, but inside there is the cry of newborns. Everyone is gathered together in Teylen's house.

Lisa and Minki have drawn a warm bath in the kitchen sink for the babies, and Sharina goes into the bathroom with Teylen, who helps her into the tub.

"Why?" Sharina cries, reaching for her mother. "Why, Mom? Chana was the only one who really understood me. She can't be gone!"

Teylen holds Sharina's hand as Sharina weeps tears into the tub water. As their hands embrace, a warmth comes into them. Teylen looks up. "Look, Rina." An image of Chana's face begins to form above the tub water, in a golden glowing orb.

"Don't cry, Sharina," Chana says. "I always knew it was going to be this way. I just couldn't put it into words. I'm happy, and I'm still here with you. Take good care of my little one. Let her play with your daughter. Keep her close. They are going to be very powerful when they grow up. Don't cry for me. I'm where I'm supposed to be. I love you." And Chana's face is gone.

Sharina looks at Teylen, and the two are silent. Then Teylen begins to sing a song and pour warm water over Sharina's beautiful black hair. Baby sounds can be heard from the other part of the house. A small *tap tap* on the bathroom door, and Minki appears with a baby in her arms.

"She wants to nurse again," Minki says, handing Sharina's baby to her.

Sharina sits up in the tub and positions her nipple into the infant's mouth.

"Collin went into town to get some breast milk from the hospital," Minki says. "Mora told him they keep a supply for when mothers pass during childbirth."

"Bring her to me," Sharina says, looking up at Minki. "Bring me Chana's baby."

Minki leaves the bathroom and returns with June, who is holding Chana's baby.

"Let me give her something," Sharina says, reaching up to the baby in June's arms. June kneels next to the tub and holds the baby at Sharina's other breast, and the infant latches on and begins nursing.

The bathroom is bathed in golden light, and outside the window, past the garden, beyond the bridge and into the forest, a golden light can be seen emanating from the ground where the afterbirths are buried. The light matches that of the uncountable stars that have appeared across the sky.

Forest animals and creatures of all kinds visit the site where the babies were born. Some lie in the grassy area that is pushed down from the group's gathering. They move about quietly, nosing the area and finding the spot where they choose to lie down. More animals come. There are deer and raccoons and even a small bear. The night is everywhere quiet, except for the owls hooting back and forth to each other across the animal-filled meadow.

E VERYONE IS JUST BEGINNING to clean up after breakfast when the large, blue van pulls into Teylen's driveway. Huang and June have left for the food co-op, and Collin, Aaron, and Paul are heading out to fix another section of fence that has a rotting four-by-four.

Everyone's attention is drawn to the large van. The door opens quickly, and Sean Webb steps out of the vehicle. "Hey Guys," he says with a wave as he heads toward Teylen peeking through the kitchen window.

Paul looks at the license plate of the vehicle: "BYEDOD."

"Sean," Paul says, smiling, as he moves toward his friend. "Love the vanity plate." Collin and Aaron join Paul in greeting Sean. The men all shake hands and give each other a man hug.

"I heard there was some work to be done out this way," Sean says as he reaches into the sliding door of the van and pulls out a huge duffel bag. "Let me put this in my trailer and I'll come help you guys."

Teylen opens the window and calls through the screen. "Hello, Mr. Webb. Hope you've come to stay this time."

Sean waves at Teylen again. "I've come to stay this time," he calls back. "May I?" he says, pointing to the trailer.

"We told you it's yours whenever you came back," Teylen replies. "Glad it's going to be occupied."

Sean heads over to the trailer. "Webb's home," the sign still reads. He tosses the duffel bag inside and heads off with Paul, Aaron, and Collin, taking in all the latest news. He already knows that Chana had been "lifted," and he has some information of his own to share with Paul and the others. Some new magnetic force on Earth is wreaking havoc on the DOD's weaponry. They haven't even been able to get their fighter planes off the ground, but then neither has anyone else on Earth. Sean rolls up his sleeves as he picks up the shovel to dig around the rotting pole. "And Washington is having a fit trying to get their computers to hang on to any data that has to do with the military," he says.

"Did they question the five guys after they returned?" Paul asks.

"They couldn't. The agents couldn't remember anything about what had happened, or even where they had been. My boss just about had an aneurysm when they came back blank."

The men have a good laugh over the tales Sean has returned with.

Inside the barn, Minki and Sharina are lying on a grouping of pillows, playing with the babies. Sharina has just nursed them and they are both heavy-lidded and ready to sleep.

"Go ahead," Minki says. "Get out and take a walk. I'll watch over them while they sleep." And the babies lie on the large pillows with cherub-like faces of contentment.

"Are you sure?" Sharina asks.

"I've got this!" Minki insists. "Go!"

Sharina gets up off the yoga loft floor and heads down the stairs and across the garden area. She takes careful steps over the footbridge and strolls into the forest behind the house. Walking over to where the afterbirths were buried, she touches the small maple tree that the men had planted on top. *It's growing quickly before winter sets in,* she thinks to herself.

"I miss you," Sharina says to the air. "You were so wonderful to have as a friend." She sits for a moment longer, listening to the water rush by and the birds singing in the trees. "She's doing great, Chana. She's growing so fast, and I'll probably only be able to nurse them another couple of months before we'll have to supplement it with something. She's a chowhound, just like you." Sharina laughs quietly out her nose, remembering how Chana loved to eat as much as she did. "I named my girl 'Telaya,' after mom, but June hasn't come up with a name for your baby yet."

As Sharina sits by the tree, she closes her eyes and breathes in the sweetness of oncoming fall. In the darkness behind her eyelids, one word appears in light: JORDAN. Sharina opens her eyes. "Are you sure, Chana?" She sits quietly, closes her eyes again, and listens. Nothing. *Maybe I just made that up in my mind,* Sharina thinks.

As she starts to get up, her eyes become level with the tag on the tree that was planted over the afterbirth. It reads, "*Acer Shireswanum* / Jordan Maple / Full Moon Maple."

"Okay," Sharina says to the air. Jordan it is, I guess." She remembers back to some of the fun times Chana and she had spent working on the farms and going into town. She looks down the river toward the rocks where they had sat fishing and Chana had caught the two big trout. Those days had filled a space of play that Sharina had missed out on, growing up.

"I miss you," Sharina says again, directing her gaze to the place of assumption. The group had built a small stone monument at that spot. "And I love you," she says as she turns to walk back toward home.

As Sharina enters the kitchen, Teylen says there is a package for her on the table. Sharina picks up the small box and reads where it is from: *Jordan, Montana*. She looks up at the ceiling. "Okay, okay, I get it!" She turns to Teylen. "Chana's baby's name is Jordan."

"Oh, you must have also spoken to June this morning," Teylen says. But Sharina had not bumped into June before she left for the food co-op.

"Why do you say that, Mom?" Sharina asks.

"Because she was up super early telling me that Chana had come to her and told her in a dream that the baby's name was *Jordan*."

Sharina smiles. "Well then, that settles it. Jordan and Telaya. Maybe Tellie for short?"

Teylen crinkles her nose at the nickname.

"Okay, *Telaya*," Sharina says, bringing her mother into her arms. They hug each other in the middle of the kitchen, accompanied by the sounds of the radio playing lightly and the men laughing in the side yard while they repair the fence.

"Funny how life has a plan for us sometimes that isn't of our own making," Sharina says into Teylen's ear.

Teylen pulls back. "Do you hear that, Rina?"

Sharina listens. She can faintly hear Minki calling.

Both women run out the door to the barn. There is golden light pouring out the windows up above. Quickly up the barn steps, they open the door at the top. Inside the yoga loft, neither of them can believe what they're seeing.

"They were asleep, and then they just touched each other's hand and this happened!" Minki says, somewhat exasperated. The babies are hovering over her head and laughing. The room is filled with golden light.

Lisa comes up the steps and into the room. "What was all the yelling about?" she says, and then, looking up, she understands.

"Jordan and Telaya have some pretty powerful abilities, for babies," Sharina says, looking at Teylen.

"Pretty powerful for *anyone*," Teylen says, and walks over to stand under the babies. "Sha, come here." She motions for Sharina to move into the middle of the room under the babies. "Touch my hand."

Sharina touches Teylen's hand. The babies begin to descend from above them, lightly landing themselves back on their pillows.

"Well!" Lisa says, walking toward the babies. "This ought to make things interesting over the next few years!"

The women all look at each other and laugh. Sharina sits down next to Jordan and Telaya. She looks at Jordan's moon-face, so much like Chana's.

Teylen, Minki, and Lisa gather close to the babies. "Maybe when they're older, they'll be able to fix things on the roof for us," Minki says, laughing.

"Or maybe they can give us a ride into town without using gas," Lisa jumps in. "Or, I know: Maybe we can use them for a trip to Hawaii that is environmentally friendly."

Teylen looks at her daughter, sitting with the miracle children. "Maybe…" she says, and she gets up to head back into the house. Sharina can hear her mother singing a familiar song on her way out.

"I am the eye in the sky, looking at you…"

CPSIA information can be obtained
at www.ICGtesting.com
Printed in the USA
JSHW081928060623
42822JS00001B/7

9 781088 127384